QUEER

The Ultimate LGBT Guide for Teens

Kathy Belge and Marke Bieschke

FOREWORD

Years ago, when we were growing up, the world was a different place. We didn't know too many other queer kids or adults. Many people felt forced to lead their lives in the closet. There were rumors, of course, like ones about the two goth boys who spent every waking moment together, or about the supposed relationship between the gym teacher Ms. Mason and the science teacher Ms. Lewis. But most people just weren't out the way they are now. Words like *gay* and *queer* were usually used as insults. The few brave kids who dared to take a same-sex date to the prom made the evening news. (They still do in some parts of the country!)

With a little luck and a lot of pride, we both made it through. We found queer friends, queer loves, and careers as writers who teach the world about the awesomeness of queer life. Our paths weren't without a few struggles, and we had to deal with a lot of confusion and discouragement. But we couldn't change who we were, and we never gave up following our dreams.

Being a queer or questioning teen still has its ups and downs. You've got to deal with coming out, trying to find your community, dating within a sometimes limited dating pool, and coping with discrimination from people who just don't get it. But if you're growing up queer today, you also have a lot to be excited about. Queer teens are coming out younger and younger, championing queer rights, starting up Gay-Straight Alliances, and, most important, talking to each other about what it means to be gay, straight, bisexual, or transgender. You're part of a whole new generation of queer and queer-friendly youth, and we wrote this book for you.

Inside, we'll talk about what it means to be queer and guide you through the stages of coming out, finding your people, dealing with haters, and scoring dates. We'll also tell you some funny (and not-so-funny!) stories about our own experiences of coming into the world as queer people. And you'll also get a taste of the rich legacy of queer art, humor, and history handed down from our queer forefathers and mothers. Queer life can be really juicy—and you're about to find out how.

Whether you're sure you're queer, wondering if you might be, or just want to know more about what it all means, this book is your ticket to a whole new rainbow-colored world.

—*Kathy Belge and Marke Bieschke*

TABLE OF CONTENTS

ONE

THE "Q" WORD

WORD

AM I QUEER?

If you're a teen, you have a lot on your plate: school, family, social drama, body issues, how to get that relative who perpetually smells like onions to stop sitting next to you at every family gathering. As if that weren't enough, some of you have one more thing to deal with—the possibility (or reality) of being queer. This realization is definitely *not* a bad thing—but it can throw you for a loop.

To best grasp what may be going on, you're going to have to spend some time looking within. That doesn't mean staring at your belly button, pondering the cosmos, the existence of God, and what Lady GaGa's going to wear next—though if any of that is helpful, go for it. But you will need to do a little soul searching.

Lots of teens—straight or queer—have questions about their sexuality. It doesn't always feel clear cut from the jump. Have you ever asked yourself any of the questions below?

- I am a girl and I have a boyfriend. But I fantasize about kissing my best girlfriend. Does that make me bisexual?

- I think anyone can be sexy, regardless of gender. What does that make me?

- I am a girl and sometimes I feel more like a guy. Does that mean I'm transgender?

- I am a guy and I keep having dreams about my girlfriend's brother. Am I gay?

If so, you probably want answers. Well, here's the good news: You don't need an answer to this today. Here's the even better news: Whatever the answer is, it's completely fine. Being straight or queer doesn't define who you are as a person. It doesn't say whether you're a good friend or a complete jerk or whether you should do ballet or go out for varsity football. It's just about who you are attracted to and, in the case of transgender people, what gender you want to live as. Any answer is the right one. And it's also OK if that answer changes at some point. It's all good.

WHAT DOES IT MEAN TO BE QUEER?

To identify as *queer* means to see yourself as being part of the LGBT community. That means you consider yourself to be lesbian, gay, bisexual, or transgender. Here's the breakdown.

Lesbian

Lesbians are women who are emotionally and sexually attracted to other women. The Greek poet Sappho, who lived during the sixth and seventh centuries, wrote about loving other women. She was born on the island of Lesbos, and this is where the term lesbian comes from.

There is no "typical" lesbian. Some lesbians consider themselves to be butch lesbians (also known as *studs*), which means they express themselves in what society might consider a masculine manner. Butch lesbians might feel more comfortable dressing in men's clothing, playing aggressive sports, working a traditionally manly job, or being the person who is more chivalrous in a relationship. *Femmes* (also known as *lipstick lesbians*), on the other hand, usually dress in a more feminine manner, wear make-up, have long hair, and enjoy activities more associated with girly-girls, like maybe shopping or watching chick flicks.

Of course, not all femmes wear lipstick, and not all butches work in construction. And some lesbians call themselves *futch*, a combination of femme and butch. There are also *blue jean femmes* (a femme who doesn't wear dresses) and *soft butches* (those who consider themselves a less hard-core form of butch). *Boi* is

ON THE QUEER FRONTIER   *AROUND 600 BC*

SWEET SAPPHO AND THE ISLE OF LESBOS

Back in ancient Greece, on the island of Lesbos, women often got together and read poetry to one another about their mutual love and devotion. A woman named Sappho was one of these poets, and although most of her poetry has been lost, she became famous because of how often her work is referenced in others' poetry. We don't know for sure if Sappho was a lesbian, but many scholars believe she was and consider her to be the pioneer of lesbian literature. The word *lesbian* itself was born from the knowledge that strong communities of women lived on Lesbos.

another term, which can indicate a hip, youthful butch who may or may not identify as trans. But remember that all of these are just labels that help lesbians clarify their social identity, and the definitions are changing even as we write this book. Not everyone uses these terms, and some people find that their relationships to masculinity and femininity change over the years. If none of these labels feel appropriate for you, feel free to make up one of your own—or go without a label altogether. These identities are really about celebrating yourself and your queerness, not bogging you down.

Uh, That Explains It (How I Knew I Was a Lesbian)

As a kid, I kept falling in love with my best friends. Sure, I had crushes on guys, but when the opportunities came to be with them or a girlfriend, I always chose the girl. When I go back and read my old journal from high school, I have to laugh at what I wrote. There are entries that say things like, "I'm not queer or anything, but I don't want Lisa to get a boyfriend because we wouldn't be able to spend as much time together" or "We're not queer or anything, but I'd just rather be with Jenny than with Joe" or "I'm not turning to girls, I just really want to be close to Kim." Seriously.

It's pretty obvious to me now that I was trying to justify what I was feeling because I was confused. At the time, I didn't really understand what it meant to be a lesbian, and the thought scared me. Lesbians were something we made fun of, and I didn't really know anyone who was openly gay.

When I got to college and started meeting other lesbians, I was finally able to admit to myself that I was queer. It was no longer some big scary thing because I was meeting some really amazing women who were lesbians. I got to see what lesbian relationships looked like and started going out dancing to lesbian bars and seeing lesbian movies. I became more and more comfortable with other lesbians and with myself. So by the time my first girlfriend, Lori, leaned in to kiss me, it felt like the most natural thing in the world.

Gay

Gay men are men who are emotionally and sexually attracted to other men. (The word gay is also used sometimes to mean homosexual in general.) Back in the day, the word gay meant "happy" or "carefree" and also the more negative "licentious," which means "lacking moral and sexual restraints." Gay began being used to describe homosexual people in the middle of the last century, though it's not totally clear why. (Maybe people thought gay people were happy to supposedly have no moral restraints!) Today, gay is usually used to describe homosexual men.

It can seem like there are as many kinds of gay men as there are kinds of music. Gay men who are into alternative rock and punk, underground art, and hipster fashion call themselves *alternaqueers*. (Lesbians and trans people can be alternaqueers, too.) Many large, hairy gay men refer to themselves as *bears*. Some younger men who pride themselves on being thin and clean shaven call themselves *twinks*. Gay men with feminine qualities might consider themselves *queens*, and when those qualities are really exaggerated, they might be called *flaming*. Gay men who work out a lot are often referred to as *muscle queens* or *gym queens* and, if they fly around the country to dance all night to circuit techno music, *circuit queens*. Wealthy gays who often dress in preppy styles are sometimes known as *A-gays*, and gay men into leather are *leathermen*. Though you'll find evidence of a lot of these subcultures online and in most major cities, you don't have to belong to any of them, and you could also create your own. Remember, these identities are only to help gay men say a little about who they are to the world. Never take on an identity if you don't want to, or let others label you against your will.

Bisexual

People who can be attracted to either sex are *bisexual*. Sometimes people think bisexuals are equally attracted to both sexes, but this is not necessarily the case. If you're open to dating both men and women, even if you prefer one sex over the other, then you can identify as bisexual (or *bi*). Sometimes people identify as bisexual during a transitional stage before coming out as lesbian or gay. For others, it truly is an identity that sticks with them their whole lives. For some people, coming out as bi is easier because it offers hope to their homophobic parents and friends that they'll end up with an opposite-sex partner some day. For others, coming out as bi is harder because people might want them to "choose" one sex or the other. If you think you may be bisexual, know that bisexuality has been around forever. Some cultures, like ancient Greece, celebrated bisexuality as a great way of life.

Pansexual

A little different than bisexuals, *pansexuals* people are attracted to not only boys and girls, but people who identify as transgender.

ON THE QUEER FRONTIER   *1993*

THE DYKES DESCEND ON DC

Every year, usually the night before the Gay Pride parades, lesbians take to their local streets in a procession of flowers, leather, motorcycles, drummers, and belly dancers to celebrate the awesomeness of being out in the world. These demonstrations are called dyke marches, and they got started in April 1993, when the National Gay and Lesbian Task Force sponsored a march on Washington for gay and lesbian rights. To make sure that a lesbian presence would be felt, political activists known as The Lesbian Avengers planned to do a women-only march the night before the main event. Word spread like wildfire, and more than 20,000 lesbians showed up to march together on April 24, 1993. That one event started an annual tradition that soon expanded to New York, Los Angeles, Chicago, Toronto, San Francisco; there was no stopping the liberated dykes of the world! Now dyke marches are a tradition in most cities. They have helped us to reclaim the word *dyke*, which was once used to insult us and now means an out-and-proud lesbian.

Transgender

People who feel there is a difference between their birth gender and the gender they truly are inside consider themselves transgender or simply trans. They often choose to live life as the gender they feel they are, or, in some cases, they don't identify as any gender at all. Transgender people sometimes opt for medical treatment—like hormones and surgery—to actually change their sex so that their bodies appear on the outside more like what they feel on the inside. People who undergo these medical procedures sometimes think of themselves as transsexuals, though often they prefer to be thought of and referred to simply as the gender they are living as (male or female) since transsexual is sometimes seen as an impersonal medical term. There are also abbreviations for people who change their sex, like FTM (female to male) or MTF (male to female), which are sometimes used.

People who feel they don't fit into either gender may use the terms gender queer or gender fluid to describe themselves. They may feel that they are neither male nor female, both male and female, or somewhere in between. They may also feel that even saying there are only two genders is too restrictive, and may identify with one of the various genderqueer terms out there like transboi, bi-gendered, or third gendered.

It's important to understand that while the identities of lesbian, gay, and bisexual refer to one's sexual orientation, being transgender does not. It is specifically about gender. People who are transgender can be straight, gay, lesbian, or bisexual.

Queer

Queer can describe people who are any of the above or people who don't want to use any of the these labels but know they fall somewhere along the LGBT spectrum or that they don't fit into the heterosexual norms.

If you find yourself wondering if any of the terms in this chapter describe you, you might be queer. Of course, you might also just be questioning—and that's OK, too. These days, we often see the acronym LGBT with a "Q" at the end (LGBTQ). That "Q" stands for *questioning*, which means people who are still figuring it out. (And aren't we all just trying to figure something out?) The "Q" can also stand for *queer*. Sometimes people even write the LGBT acronym as LGBTQQ or LGBTQQI, where the I stands for *intersex* (see page 24). With all those letters to keep track of, sometimes it's easier to just say queer!

Life's a Drag

Dressing in drag (i.e., wearing the clothing of another gender for fun, performance, or to make a statement) has long been a celebrated part of queer culture. People do it to exaggerate traditional gender roles, so they often wind up wearing things like ultra high heels or huge fake mustaches, especially in live performances. When a male performer wears women's clothing, he's called a "drag queen"; a woman performer dressing in men's clothing is called a "drag king". Often these performers lip-sync to music onstage or perform comedy routines, and the queer community (known for challenging traditional gender roles) is a big part of the drag performer fan base.

HOW DO I KNOW IF I'M QUEER?

You may have simply always felt different from other kids. Maybe the words other people use to describe themselves just don't seem to fit you, or you don't feel comfortable dressing or acting the way that society says you should. If you're a boy, maybe you're into "girl stuff." If you're a girl, maybe you're into "boy stuff." Maybe you don't feel like you're a girl *or* a boy but that you're something unique that doesn't really have a name. Maybe you're a boy into boy stuff or a girl into girl stuff, but you feel attracted to other boys or other girls.

Even if you relate to any of the above, that doesn't necessarily mean you are LGBT. Plenty of straight people are into things that most of society doesn't consider "normal" like heavy metal, contemporary art, or raspberry granola, and you certainly wouldn't base your sexuality on what you like to eat for breakfast. Besides, you're in a stage of your life right now when love can feel a bit confusing, and you may not know if you want to kiss that cute soccer player or just want to *be* her. You'll probably get crushes on all kinds of people, from teachers and best friends to celebrities and star athletes. You may even go through a period of trying out different things to find out what's right for you. Some days you might feel one way, and other days, another. Just because your friends aren't talking about conflicting feelings around sexuality doesn't mean they aren't feeling them, too.

That being said, if your feelings persist, then you may decide to start identifying as queer or as any of the related identities. If so, embrace it! Being part of the LGBT community is great, but it does mean that, yes, you are a little bit different than most of the people you know. Being different, of course, is something to celebrate. But it also means that sometimes you might feel like you are from another planet. If so, think of us as your tour guides to Planet Queer!

Reclaiming Our Words

In the last century, the words *queer*, *dyke*, and *fag* have been used to mock, shame, and intimidate LGBT people, which is really awful. In the dictionary, the word queer translates to "odd" or "weird," and people called us that because they thought it was weird to be LGBT. Likewise, dyke and fag can be used as insults. But in recent years, many LGBT people started taking these words back, turning them from negative to positive terms. Reclaiming these words started as a political act, a way of identifying ourselves as a group of people who were proud of who we were, and we continue to use these words in a loving and accepting way.

As you may have noticed, some people still try to use these words as a weapon, like if someone yells "dyke!" at you out of a car window or scrawls "queer" on your locker. But these words are fast gaining acceptance in mainstream society and being seen as positive, like in dyke marches or on the TV show *Queer Eye for the Straight Guy*. You'll usually know if someone is using a queer word in a positive or negative way by the context.

What can be a bit tricky is that the outside world doesn't always get that we in the LGBT community use words like dyke and fag amongst ourselves as terms of endearment. As a matter of fact, some schools, in their quest to be more welcoming to LGBT students, ban the use of the word queer because they only see it as an insult! (Hopefully they won't ban this book.) The schools mean well, and they're just trying to halt antiqueer activity, but we hope it's only a matter of time before everyone views all queer words in a positive light. ("Hey, do you know Marke?" "Yeah, he's that cool queer guy, right?")

DO I HAVE TO HAVE SEX TO KNOW?

Lots of questioning teens think they need to have sex to know if they are queer, and often older people will doubt a teen's assertion of being queer with a response like, "How could you know? You haven't had sex yet!" But the truth is that you don't have to have sex to know if you're LGBT. Most of the time, it's something you'll just have a sense about. For instance, if you're a guy and you consistently have crushes on other guys, then you might be gay. You don't have to act on those attractions sexually to know how you feel. Straight kids have crushes all the time and they don't need to act on them to know they are straight. It's no different for queer kids.

Some people do say that they discovered they were lesbian, gay, or bisexual after experimenting sexually. So that is possible. But most people say that if you are queer, you'll know it on a much deeper level. It becomes a part of your identity and how you see yourself. It's more about who you are and who you have feelings toward rather than simply who you're getting busy with.

On the flip side, just because you've had sex with some-one of the same gender, you're not necessarily gay or lesbian. Sometimes people experiment just for fun and still don't consider themselves queer because they don't want to actually date or have relationships with people of the same gender. Or you might have fantasies or dreams about having sex with someone of the same gender, but in real life you don't feel the same way. Obviously, sex is part of the queer equation, but it's definitely not the whole thing.

WHY ARE PEOPLE QUEER?

That's the multimillion dollar question. And it's one that no one's really been able to answer yet, probably because everyone, queer or straight, is different. For years, scientists have been trying to discover if there is a "gay gene" or something in our brains that makes us prefer the same sex. So far, the studies have been inconclusive, and we don't know exactly what makes one person gay and another bisexual or trans or even straight, for that matter. There are any number of things that make you the person you are.

For some queer people, it seems like they were just born that way. For others, it's the way our emotions and sexuality developed as we grew up and our personality began expressing itself. And other people say that somewhere along the way, they just changed and suddenly started liking people of the same gender.

But though you may come into your queerness at any stage, it's not a choice. It's something that naturally happens. You can't "train" yourself to be straight any more than you can train yourself to have three eyeballs, fly like a bird, breathe underwater, or like listening to the Rolling Stones as much as your parents do. You have no control over your sexual orientation or gender identity. Be authentic and you'll gain the respect of others and yourself. You'll also be way happier in the long run.

WHERE ARE YOU ON THE SEXUAL SPECTRUM?

Back in the 1940s, a sex researcher named Alfred Kinsey asked people to be honest about their sexual activities, fantasies, and romantic attractions. After thousands of interviews, he found that it is rare that a person is solely homosexual or heterosexual. People's desires and preferences fell all along what he called a "sexual spectrum" (also known as the Kinsey Scale) between gay and straight. What he interpreted this to mean was that most humans have the capability to be attracted to or to fall in love with both men and women. We think that the idea of viewing sexuality

What Is Intersex?

People who are *intersex* are born with sexual anatomy that doesn't match typical male or female anatomy. There are many varieties of intersex, some of which show up at birth and others that appear at puberty. In some cases, intersex people can go the majority of their lives—or even their entire lives—not knowing they are intersex. Estimates are that 1 in 100 births result in some form of intersexism, where the body is different from the standard male or female. For example, a girl might be born with a large clitoris or no vaginal opening, or a boy might have a scrotum that is divided so it looks more like a labia. Some doctors will also consider someone to be intersex if they have both ovarian and testicular tissue. Of course, what's most important is how intersex people view themselves. They may have a male or female gender identity or neither. However, the social pressures to fit into a specific gender can be confusing and harmful and even result in unnecessary genital reassignment surgeries to "correct" something that was perfectly healthy to begin with. The important thing to remember is that if you are intersex, you are perfect just as you are and a welcome part of the queer community (though not all intersex people identify with the queer community, which is totally fine). If you want to learn more, read the books on intersexuality mentioned in the Resources section.

as a spectrum is a great way to look at it. It means there is some fluidity in our preferences, and everything is totally acceptable.

Of course, that doesn't mean you won't prefer to date one gender or the other. You probably will. But if you're not sure how to label yourself or where you fall on the spectrum of straight, bi, or gay/lesbian, we say don't stress about it. Even though it may seem like everyone around you has it figured out, they proably don't. Instead, see all of your questions about your sexuality as something that makes your life more interesting and will give you more personal insight and confidence.

Want to try a little experiment? Look at the scale below and locate where you think you are on the spectrum. Make a note of what you think today, and then see if it's the same a year from now.

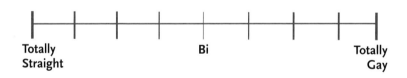

Totally Straight   **Bi**   **Totally Gay**

My Big Gay Revelation

For me, the signs were probably there from the start. I was the kind of little kid who played dress-up in his mom's clothes, ran around singing show tunes at the top of his voice, and pretend-flirted with other boys. (My parents even have pictures of me kissing one of my boy cousins on the lips when we were in diapers!) In grade school, I also fooled around with some other boys in my neighborhood and from my school. But I didn't really think about it in terms of whether I was gay or straight or whatever. I knew lots of boys who did stuff like this, and it didn't seem like a big deal.

It wasn't until around sixth grade, when I started developing deep crushes on other boys, that I started thinking I might be a little different. But I still couldn't put my finger on it. I had never even heard the word gay until some older boys from another school tried to insult me by calling me that. I did a little research in the library to find out more and discovered a whole history of people who not only had sex with people of the same gender but had passionate romantic relationships as well. In fact, there was an entire community of people who felt the same way I did; it was a delicious wonderland of queerness! I realized it was OK to like other boys in "that way," and even though it took a little while to find other boys who liked me back, I knew that I wasn't "abnormal" or "weird"—just a little bit different.

THE "Q" WORD: AM I QUEER?

ONE

WHEN DO I NEED TO DECIDE IF I'M QUEER?

There is no time limit. Like we said, it's natural to go through a period of questioning and experimenting before you know what's right for you. You may spend some time being *bi-curious*, which means you wonder a lot about what it would be like to get with someone of your own gender. You may try out dressing as the opposite gender or explore your feelings by looking at photos or movies to see what appeals to you. It's your life. Only you can decide when and how to express your gender identity and sexuality—no one else.

What Percentage of the Population Is Queer?

As you can imagine, determining someone's sexual orientation or gender identity is not an easy task. Numerous studies and polls have been done over the years, but the results have varied. Accuracy can depend on what questions are asked, how safe the respondents feel in answering them, whether the people answering the questions are out or being honest, and how one even defines queer. Some people engage in same-sex sexual behavior but don't identify as queer. Some people may not be out yet or may not feel comfortable answering questions about queerness. Most researchers these days use the general estimate of 10 percent, but some say that, because of the above issues with the studies, it could be as high as 20 percent. The truth is, we may never know for sure what percentage of the population is queer.

TWO

EMBRACING YOUR QUEERNESS

COMING OUT

OK, so you've looked in your heart and realized you're queer. Applause moment! Big ups from us for being honest with yourself.

But it can also be a little overwhelming. We know—we went through it, too. There's so much information, so much to explore. It's like you just got a big gay Xbox for your birthday and you need to figure out how to work the controls. What does that button do? What happens when I push the joystick this way? How can I show off my optimum gaming skills?

Don't go getting your tighty-whiteys (or teeny bikinis) all in a twist. The first important thing you should know is that everything's going to be all right.

Some things may be different than before, but other things won't change at all. What's cool is that you now belong to a giant family of other LGBT people. We don't use a rainbow as our symbol just because of the pretty colors. We use it because it stretches across the sky, connecting all kinds of people. You're plugged in to a fascinating culture, where everyone is unique but they all share something special. Don't be afraid to reach out for support or to offer your advice to others.

One of the things you're probably wondering is if you should let anyone know that you're LGBT. This is known as *coming out,* and it's a unique process for everyone. While you might think of coming out as an external process where you stand on a platform and announce to the world that you're queer, it's quite the opposite; the first person you will come out to is actually yourself. You may sit with this knowledge for a while before you decide to tell anyone else. Or sometimes a close friend or counselor helps you figure it out. But eventually, you'll feel confident enough to look in the mirror and say to yourself, "I'm queer. And I'm also sexy as hell." Well, you might not say that second part, but you are, and you should know it.

Of course, most people aren't going to run outside right away, waving their arms in the air like Elmo the Homo and screaming, "Hey, Ma! Guess what? I'm queer!" Coming out to your friends and family can be a gradual process, which might be good if you don't want to be fielding your mother's questions about your sex life and your uncle Joe's fear that you won't carry on the family name all at once. Feel free to take some time to figure out how you want to handle spreading the news. Some teens tell certain people at certain times or tell others only on a need-to-know basis. Others can't wait to share the news with everyone. Figure out which path is appropriate for your own journey, and blaze it when you're ready.

Hi me! I'm queer.

How Kathy Came Out to Her Parents

I was 19 and I was traveling cross-country (by foot!) to join a group of people working on peace and justice issues. I was a young and proud lesbian, and everyone around me knew I was gay—but not my family back home. The more time I spent being out in my new environment, the worse I felt about the fact that I wasn't out to my parents. So one day I decided to sit down and write them a letter. In it, I tried to explain that I was a lesbian and probably always had been. I said that I saw myself making a life with another woman and that I was happy the way I was and hoped they would be, too. I put a stamp on it and sent it off.

There was no way for my parents to call me, but I was able to receive mail at various post offices along my route. My dad's letter came first. In it he said he was fearful that I would have a hard life but he loved me no matter what and only wanted me to be happy. My mom's letter, which followed, said the Kathy she knew "was dead" and that she was going to need some time to adjust to the news. I remember sitting in my tent and bawling my eyes out.

Once I finally got up the courage to call home, my Mom was able to explain what she meant: that she had to let go of all her old preconceptions about me and start to look at me as a new person. I was relieved but still wished I had told my parents in person so we could have had a real discussion about it. Now that it's many years later, both of my parents are totally fine with my being queer and they are glad that part of my job is to help other people come out and feel OK about it.

COMING OUT TO YOUR FAMILY

A lot of parents get freaked out when they find out that one of their children is LGBT—even if they're the most loving and supportive parents in the world. Many older folks immediately think about the "sex" part of homosexuality or bisexuality, though you may not be thinking about that at all. For instance, you might just be trying to talk to a crush without chewing all of your nails off, but your parents are already envisioning what you'll be doing in bed together.

To be fair, most parents are uncomfortable with any thoughts that involve their kids and sex, even if the kids are straight. Parents worry about things like disease, heartbreak, and pregnancy—it's their job. But if they know that their kid is queer, they'll find new things to be concerned about, like what the neighbors will think, if it means they won't have grandchildren, or if all their ambitious plans for you will suddenly fall apart.

We know these fears are complete nonsense. No one knows what the future will bring. And who cares what the neighbors think about your personal life? But a lot of adults were taught when they were younger that being queer is always a negative thing. You'll need to educate yourself and channel some confidence to be able to calm their fears and speak your truth. It may take a lot of effort for you to convince them that you're totally fine with who you are and that your life is not over. (*Au contraire*—it's just beginning!) And who knows? Maybe your parents will give you a giant bear hug and thank you for being honest. Or maybe they've known all along, didn't think it was a big deal, and were just waiting for you to admit it. In that case, your coming out will actually relieve them.

Some queer teens prefer to tell a close brother or sister first (and sometimes your brothers and sisters figure it out for you, even before you know yourself). Other queer teens approach an aunt, uncle, or cousin with whom they share a special bond. Telling someone you trust in your family before you tell your parents can be good practice. It will help give you the courage to come out to your folks and build a safety net in case your parents react badly.

You may feel ready to jump right in and tell your folks that you're LGBT. But before you let the games begin, ask yourself, "Is this the right time?" If you're not totally sure if you're queer and are still in the questioning stage, then sometimes it's best to wait until you're certain before you make any declarations. There's no use stirring up a potential hornet's nest until necessary, and it'll be easier to reassure your parents if you yourself feel confident. Of course, if you have the kind of relationship with your parents where you can talk openly about things and you think they'd be able to help you process your feelings without judgment, then you can share what's going on for you. You know your parents best, so do what works for you. And if you feel they really have to know *right now*, be prepared for their responses.

HOW TO DO IT

You've decided you're going to do it: You're going to tell your folks that you're as queer as a three-dollar bill with a picture of Liberace on it. Think about these three factors as you're planning your course of action.

◎ **Timing is everything.** Pick a time that you know you can talk to them uninterrupted. It's best not to do this around a family holiday, but if one of your parents lives far away and that's the only time you see them, then work with what you have. Some people like to sit their parents down and make an announcement. For others, it feels more comfortable to talk while you're doing something else, like making dinner or folding laundry. If your parents are separated, you may need to do this twice, so start with the one you think will take it better and use his or her reaction to gauge how and when to approach the other parent.

And don't bring along your boyfriend or girlfriend. You want to make sure your parents understand that this is about who you are, not about the person you happen to be dating at the moment.

 **Plan it out.** Some people just blurt out the news with little finesse, but that's not necessarily the best idea because it can seem confrontational. Instead, give some thought to what you are going to say and how you are going to say it. Need some help? Start by telling your parents that you have something important you want to tell them. Assure them you've done a lot of thinking and reflecting about it, and that you've realized that you're lesbian, gay, bi, or trans. Tell them you feel good about coming out to them because you know they appreciate honesty and that you hope the family can support you.

If you are really nervous about it, you could try writing down what you want to say in advance and practice the scene with a friend. See if he or she can ask you some difficult questions, and practice answering them.

ON THE QUEER FRONTIER   *1997*

YEP. I'M GAY

In 1997, Ellen DeGeneres, a popular TV star, changed the landscape of queer representation on TV and the perception of queer actors in the public eye. At the time, DeGeneres had her own show called *Ellen* (a sitcom in which she played the main character), and in an historic episode, she had her character, Ellen Morgan, come out as a lesbian on the show. While there had already been TV shows with gay or lesbian characters, the characters often felt stereotyped, and the parts were small. Now there was a protagonist on prime time TV talking openly about being a lesbian, which was really exciting for queer viewers. At the same time, DeGeneres herself also decided to come out to the public. She announced to the world that she was a lesbian on the cover of *Time* magazine. (The famous headline was "Yep. I'm Gay.") She received backlash from conservatives for both of these moves, but in the end, her coming out inspired other queer celebrities and their fans to become more open about their sexuality. DeGeneres also broke new ground in the way queerness was treated on mainstream shows. Years later, shows like *Will and Grace, Brothers and Sisters, Glee*, and *Greek* would feature queer protagonists and draw huge audiences.

◉ **Be patient.** Give your parents time to react. Be prepared to answer any questions they have. You can arm yourself with some literature from the helpful organization Parents, Families, and Friends of Lesbians and Gays (PFLAG, pflag.org), if you think that will help. If your parents are religious, you might want to line up a gay-friendly priest, rabbi, imam, or other religious leader to talk to them, or offer some literature that addresses homosexuality and religion. (See our Resources section.) Try to let them know that nothing has changed about you, that they just know something new about you that they didn't before. Offer to talk more about it later if they need time to take it all in. Hopefully you'll start a continuing dialogue and things will grow positively from there.

HELP THEM OUT

If your parents react badly, it's likely because they are a little scared and just looking for a way to understand what's happening. It may feel a little annoying to have to take care of their needs at a time when you're going through so much yourself, but if there's any way you can help them (short of pretending you're someone else!), try to do it. For instance, maybe you can suggest they talk to other gay-friendly people in the family or gay friends or neighbors.

Also, try to stay calm and offer to answer any questions they may have as best you can. Here are some things they may ask.

Are you sure?

How do you know?

Is it a phase?

What about grandchildren?

But then why did you date (insert opposite sex person's name here) last year!

What did I do wrong?

Are you just saying this because we won't buy you a new laptop for your birthday?

Let them know that times have changed and being gay doesn't necessarily mean that you're going to be the last kid picked for kickball anymore or that the football players are going to shove you into the lockers. Plenty of LGBT kids and adults are doing just fine in the world. Just look at Ellen DeGeneres, T. R. Knight, and Clay Aiken. If your parents are politically and socially conservative, you may want to point out that former Vice President Dick Cheney's daughter Mary is an out lesbian who has her father's support, or that both Republican Sen. John McCain's wife Cindy and daughter Meghan are activists for same-sex marriage. Do some research beforehand (see our Resources section in the back of the book) and be ready to give your family a list of recommendations to help them educate themselves.

And if your parents are just losing it, suggest that you continue the conversation when everyone's had time to digest your announcement. They may need to go talk amongst themselves for a moment or express their emotions to an uninvolved friend. Giving them space shows that you're mature enough to handle the whole coming out thing.

HAVE A BACKUP PLAN

Some parents get *really* upset when they find out their kid is gay, lesbian, bi, or trans. Like *really* upset. So as lame as it is that you even have to think about this, you may want to devise a little backup plan if things don't go so well and you need a quick getaway. Hopefully your parents aren't going to turn into giant homophobic Transformers and blow up the world when they hear you like other girls or guys, but better safe than sorry. Is there someone—a best friend, an aunt, your taekwondo teacher—who you could stay with for a while or who could offer you some support? We don't want to make you all worried, but if you do decide to spill your gay guts to your parents, weaving yourself a safety net might make you feel more secure.

No matter how your parents react, you should be prepared for things to be a little different around the house for a while. Some parents will act like nothing has happened and hope that it will all go away. Others might act overly nice to show how accepting they are. Others may not look you in the eye for a while, or try to do things to get you to change. They might think they did something wrong that caused you to be gay. (There are actually still people out there who believe a domineering mother or absent father can "turn" people gay!) You might have to renegotiate things like hanging out with friends or having friends in your room. Try to be patient. It probably took you awhile to realize and accept that you are queer, and it's probably also going to take your parents some time to get used to the idea.

YOU'RE NOT READY BUT THEY ARE

What if your parents question you about your sexual orientation or your relationship with your girlfriend or boyfriend before you are ready to talk about it? Do you *have* to tell them everything? Not if you don't want to. It's a good idea to let your parents know where you

ON THE QUEER FRONTIER

2010

MILITARY BRASS

Even though the military needs every good soldier it can get, it has been banning gays from serving since 1916. In an effort to protect gays from being discharged, President Bill Clinton instituted a policy known as Don't Ask, Don't Tell in 1992. The military was not supposed to ask, and soldiers weren't supposed to talk, about a soldier's sexual orientation. But still, military "witch hunts" continued, and more than 13,000 service members have since been discharged for being gay. Besides that, the policy unfairly kept queer soldiers in the closet. Fed up with having to live a lie, Lt. Dan Choi came out on a TV news program on March 19, 2009. Despite being a West Point graduate and Iraq veteran who is fluent in Arabic (he was one of only eight soldiers from his graduating class who majored in Arabic), he was *still* discharged. Choi has since become an advocate for LGBT rights in the military, and others, including some politicians, have since joined the fight to change the situation, knowing that being a good soldier has nothing to do with one's sexual orientation.

are when you go out so they can be sure that you're not in any danger. But that doesn't mean you need to tell them that you are LGBT until you are ready. So if you are still feeling protective about your new identity, do your best to gently deflect questions that feel too invasive. That being said, people often ask about things because they're ready to listen to the answer. If they're asking in more of a curious way than in a hostile way, it might be a good opportunity for you to talk to them about it.

YOU'RE OUTED

Sometimes you don't have the luxury of telling your parents you're gay or trans; they find out without your help. Maybe you're spotted holding hands with or kissing your boyfriend or girlfriend. Or maybe your mom finds text messages about your last date or your gym teacher calls home and asks one of your parents why you are binding your breasts. Maybe your dad finds some of your magazines, and they're pretty obviously for a queer audience.

If something like this happens to you, it's totally normal to feel upset and even betrayed. But knowing that your reaction is normal probably won't help as you sit at your kitchen table, listening

to your parents say, "Is there anything you need to tell us?" It probably wasn't your plan to come out to your parents in this way, but there's nothing you can do about it now.

If you were planning on coming out anyway, this might be a good time to do it, particularly if your parents are acting more curious and compassionate than angry and hysterical. Of course, if you feel you need to protect your safety, either physical or emotional, it's OK to be evasive. Tell your parents you were just joking or it must have been someone else's. If that doesn't work, resort to your backup plan (see page 41).

YOU'RE ASKED TO KEEP IT A SECRET

Sometimes when you come out to your parents, they'll ask that you not tell other members of your family or the neighbors until your parents have had time to think. If you've already told other family members, you should let your parents know and then offer not to spread the news any further until you and your parents can talk more. That way they won't feel ganged up on.

But you need to set clear limits on their coming out moratorium. If your parents never give you the go-ahead to tell other people, you could wind up still being stuck in the closet 15 years down the road, unable to tell your grandmother about your life partner or bring a date to big family events. That's not going to feel good to anyone, including your future partners. So it's good to give your parents a little time to get accustomed to the idea—but not a whole lifetime.

YOUR PARENTS WON'T
ACCEPT THE TRUTH

So you've come out to your parents, and they're not willing to accept it. It can be frustrating to live in a situation where you feel you don't have the freedom to be yourself—to date who you want, to wear the outfits you want, to hang out with your friends, or simply to talk, walk, and express yourself in your natural way. But they are still your parents, and they still have power over you. What do you do?

Sometimes it just takes parents awhile to get used to things. Let them sit with the information for a bit before you start asking their permission for things that make them uncomfortable. Then slowly reintroduce the idea by letting them know about someone you like or a date you'd like to go on and see if, over time, they become more permissive.

If they don't, remember that straight teens find ways to spend time together even if their parents disapprove. Your parents may have even had to sneak off when they were teens to meet the person they liked. Of course, if your parents are really strict, you may just have to wait it out. Eighteen may seem like an eternity away, but eventually you'll get there and then you can make your own decisions. Living your life in secret (or not really living it at all) can be frustrating, but don't make any rash decisions. A restricted life at home may be bad, but life on the streets is certainly no picnic.

COMING OUT AT SCHOOL

Should you or shouldn't you come out at school? Will everyone laugh at you? Or will they just shrug and say, "Yeah, so?" Sometimes it's hard to say. Here are some things to consider before you come out.

⊚ **Is your school a place you'd feel comfortable coming out?** Some schools are certainly more liberal (and safer) to come out in than others. While it's important that you don't have to live in secrecy, it's more important that you actually live through high school. See if you can find other LGBT allies at school, and weigh your options accordingly.

⊚ **Who do you want to come out to?** Even if you only come out to one person, and even if he or she seems trustworthy, there is always a chance that you might be outed to the whole school. Make sure you can really trust the person you tell to keep a secret or that you're ready for everyone to find out.

⊚ **Are you ready to handle some rejection?** It's freeing to come out—who doesn't want to live authentically?—but you should be prepared for some rejection and maybe even harassment. Your friends might get weird after you tell them. They may be afraid that people will judge them for being friends with you, or they may even think you will now start coming on to them! In most cases, people just need time to process it all, but sometimes you will lose someone close to you. Of course, you might not want a friend who won't accept you, but at the same time, it can be hard to lose all of your friends at once, which does happen for some people. So it's an important thing to consider.

Before you come out to people, you might want to test the waters a bit, to see how they feel about LGBT people in general. Assess the situation. Your friends may be giant homophobes or the biggest gay rights cheerleaders this side of Margaret Cho. How can you find out? Even before you come out to people, it's pretty easy to tell if they're gay-friendly or not. Just figure out a way to bring up the issue in conversation. "Did you hear they're going to start marrying gay people in our church? What do you think about that?" "Billy Jones just called Orlando a faggot. That pisses me off." "If I hear 'no homo' one more time, I'm going to scream." Listen to how they respond, and then decide whether or not you feel comfortable coming out to them.

HOW TO DO IT

So you've decided to come out to a friend. How do you actually utter the words? It will likely depend on the closeness of your friendship, and your own communication style. Here are two suggestions.

✪ Tell your friend you'd like to talk to them about something in private. This is a good way to let them know something important is on your mind. Warning: This can also make it seem like you're about to say some big bad thing, and your friend might get nervous. The up side is that when you say you're just queer, your friend might actually be relieved!

✪ Just let it slip into conversation. When the boys are talking about the girls they like, say that you think another guy is hot. Or say you wish your school had a Gay-Straight Alliance (GSA) because you would attend. (More about GSAs on pages 61 and 72.) If you can do it this way, it normalizes the situation and doesn't make it seem like a big deal. (Because it's really not.)

If you are only at the stage of questioning your sexual orientation, it can be helpful to talk to a close friend about what you're going through. You can even ask your friend questions about himself or herself in order to introduce the topic. For instance, if you are trans, you might start the conversation off with, "Have you ever wished you were a boy (or girl)?" Not only is this a good way to get into a conversation, but it's also a good segue into talking about yourself.

On the Streets

If your parents are not accepting who you are, or maybe someone at home is just plain abusive, you may think about packing up and leaving. But think things through before you decide to leave. Life on the streets is really rough. And once you become homeless, it can be really hard to work your way back into society. If you find yourself in an unbearable situation, first investigate your other options, like staying with a friend's family or a relative. If all that fails and you do find yourself on the streets (or if your parents actually put you there), make your way to a social services agency (see Resources section) that can help you work things out with your family or, if that's not possible, help you find housing, stay in school, and possibly get a job. According to the National Gay and Lesbian Task Force, up to 42 percent of homeless teens surveyed in 2006 identified as gay or lesbian and others identified as bisexual or transgender. Many of these teens were likely facing rejection or even abuse at home because of their sexuality. Reach out and get the help you need so you don't become a statistic yourself.

CARVING OUT YOUR NEW IDENTITY

Now that you're out, you might feel the urge to go buy those spandex short-shorts and sprinkle glitter on your eyelashes. Or you might cut your hair just like Tegan and Sara and start wearing nothing but rainbow T-shirts. That's cool. Style is a big part of who you are as a teen, and it's important to express yourself. But don't think you have to follow any particular stereotype.

You may be a lesbian who is a girly girl who loves makeup and shopping for lacy underwear, or a gay boy who only wears khakis and loves to play lacrosse. You don't have to play into a stereotype or conform to "gay" fashion if it doesn't feel like you. And if other LGBT kids your age are giving you grief for looking or behaving straight, just laugh it off and remember this wise statement Kathy once saw scrawled on a bathroom wall: "You laugh at me because I'm different. I laugh at you because you're all the same." It's enough to have to deal with getting criticized by straight people for not being like them; you certainly don't need to deal with that from the queer community!

GAY & GORGEOUS

IF THINGS DON'T GO WELL

Coming out to yourself—and to others—is not the easiest thing for anyone, much less someone in high school who's already dealing with tons of other stress. If your parents don't accept you, it can make you feel pretty crappy. Or maybe *you* don't want to be gay and wish you could change. Or the kids at school are treating you like last year's jeans. If you're feeling bummed, it's pretty normal to cry for a few days, retreat to your room, and not answer your cell phone or email. But if, after a week, dressing up the family dog as a Vegas showgirl still doesn't cheer you up, you may want to get some help. And if you're doing something like cutting yourself to try to make the pain inside go away, you definitely need to talk to someone. Cutting will not make the root cause of your pain go away, and until you address the root cause, you're not going to truly feel better. Ultimately, you need to find a way to accept—and really love—who you are.

Coming Out to a Crush

Many times we're tempted to come out first to the person we have a crush on. If the feelings are mutual, that can be an awesome thing. But if they're not, you risk not only some awkward moments but also putting a strain on your friendship—especially if you're not even sure whether your crush is queer or queer-friendly. Just be prepared for either. If you get rejected, don't make it more than it is: a single (not lifetime) rejection. Although it may suck at the time, it'll make you stronger.

FINDING A QUEER-POSITIVE COUNSELOR

It's a mature step to reach out to a professional; just make sure that your therapist is queer-friendly! The last thing you want to do is go to a therapist who has never met an LGBT person or has the goal of "reforming" you to be straight (see page 55). If you even suspect either of these things about your prospective therapist, look for someone else. Here are some ways to find queer-positive therapists:

- **The internet.** You can just Google "youth LGBT therapist" (along with your ZIP code or city) and see what comes up. Counselors who specialize in LGBT issues will post that on their websites.

- **A local LGBT center.** If you live in a city with an LGBT center, call and ask if it has a list of queer-friendly therapists.

- **Queer-friendly publications.** Look at ads in local LGBT publications, like alternative or gay newspapers or an LGBT phonebook.

- **Insurance plans.** If your parents' or your insurance plan gives you a list of therapists, call ahead and see who has experience working with LGBT teens.

Don't get discouraged if you don't find the right therapist on your first shot. Sometimes you have to go through a few before you find one that really works for you.

In some cases, your parents are the ones who want you to go to therapy, not you. They think that because you are gay or trans, you might need someone to talk to. Even if you don't feel like going, give it a shot at least once or twice. Talking to someone about what's going on with you can be really helpful—as long as they don't try to change you.

TALKING TO OTHER PEOPLE

Perhaps you don't want or need to go to a professional counselor, but you do want to talk to someone who isn't going to judge you and can give an unbiased opinion. Peer counseling can be a great option in this instance. Peer counselors are other teens who have been trained to listen and help you sort through your thoughts and feelings. Peer counseling programs are offered at some high schools, LGBT community centers, and other teen programs.

Suicide

LGBT teens are more likely than straight teens to attempt suicide. Some studies show that up to 40 percent of gay teens and 39 percent of lesbian youth attempt suicide at some point. This is not because they are queer; it's because they are having a hard time dealing with how society treats them for being queer. Suicide is not the answer. If you are feeling suicidal—or think a friend is—talk to a trusted friend, parent, teacher, counselor, or coach. Check out The Trevor Project (thetrevorproject.org), which is an organization for queer teens that has a 24-hour help line (see Resources section).

IN MARKE'S WORDS

How I Came Out at School

All of my friends in grade school knew I liked boys, and whenever anyone tried to bully me by calling me gay, everyone else just laughed and said, "Of course he is, duh!" But then I enrolled in an all-boys high school with only a few of my old friends. I made no attempt to hide the fact that I was gay, but I never declared it outright either. The guys I dated went to other schools, and I took girls to formal dances because they were my best friends and I knew we'd have a blast together.

Then, during my sophomore year, something happened that changed everything. I was sitting at the lunch table with friends, and this jerky guy came up to the table and said, "OK, Marke, time to admit it. Tell everyone that you're a fag." At first we all laughed at how ridiculous it sounded, but then everyone's eyes turned to me, and I realized I had to say something. I'd never officially come out, but it seemed like now or never. So I took a deep breath and said with a shrug, "I prefer the term gay."

Things got a little strange after that. Now that it was out in the open, some of my friends turned a cold shoulder to me for a while, afraid that they'd somehow be tainted socially by knowing me. That didn't last long, but it hurt. They eventually realized that I was the same person I'd always been and that hanging out with me didn't change anything about their social status—the people who liked them still liked them, and the people who didn't still didn't. Did everyone look at me in class whenever something remotely gay came up? Yes. So I just made sure I looked great and tried to handle everything with style. It was a little lonely being the only out person in my school. But soon enough, a couple of questioning guys came to me for advice, and I found out that I wasn't the only one after all.

Sometimes the best person to talk to is a friend or sibling, since they often know you best. But remember that people close to you may advise you to do what *they* would do, which isn't always the same as what's best for *you*. Also, some problems, like abuse, depression, eating disorders, or drug and alcohol addicitons need to be dealt with by a skilled professional.

WHEN PEOPLE TRY TO UN-QUEER YOU

No one can change the fact that you're queer. But some adults may freak out about it and try to change you through "reparative therapy," also called "conversion therapy." This is when a counselor or therapist attempts to "make you straight," a practice that is denounced by the American Psychological Association. It's a cruel, discriminatory tactic that usually ends up causing the person receiving "treatment" a lot of unnecessary con-fusion and pain. No amount of trying to imagine that you're straight or practicing "methods" designed to make you feel bad about yourself will change you — but this kind of therapy *can* screw you up. For one, you may start to hate who you are. And you are likely to get frustrated with trying really hard to change and not being able to.

If your parents want to take you to a reparative thera-pist, don't agree to it. There is nothing wrong with being LGBT! Offer instead to see a queer-friendly therapist, and let them know you'd even be willing to see one together.

THREE

NAVIGATING YOUR QUEER SPHERE

FINDING YOUR PEOPLE

If you've ever seen shows like The *L Word* or *Queer As Folk*, watched the Logo TV channel, read the Rainbow Boys series, or listened to Sirius OutQ radio, you've started to learn that there are certain aspects of being queer that are universal. We sometimes grow up feeling different, but once we discover our community, we learn that our differences are shared with other LGBTs. No matter if you're in East LA or Eastport, Maine, you're likely to find lesbians with short hair who love sports, and gay men who tried on their mother's dresses when they were kids. Yes, those are stereotypes, but they're also part of our culture. Where would Broadway be without gay men? How would the WNBA survive without lesbians?

However, that doesn't mean you have to give up any part of your unique self in order to be queer. Not every gay guy wants to be a floral designer or sing along to *Glee*. Not every lesbian shaves her head or listens to Brandi Carlile. Everyone is different. Lesbians can drool over Jimmy Choo heels, gay men can play professional rugby, and trans women can go dancing at gay clubs. All of this variety is part of LGBT culture, and you can have a blast carving out your own particular niche in it. Do things sometimes get confusing? Well, yes. But you're not alone in your queer exploration; there are millions and millions of other LGBT folks testing out different identities and expressing themselves in their own special ways.

That's what's so cool about being queer: You have an incredible culture to explore and a huge community of people to explore it with. The possibilities for connection are endless. LGBT culture and community extends back throughout history in the form of stories, poetry, art, and music—even though it's taken awhile for it to come out in the open. When you're young and queer, you may spend a lot of time thinking you're the only one. It can be such a relief to finally find others who get your sense of style, who know what it's like to be different, and who you can talk to about anything without being judged or feeling out of place. There's a whole bunch of people waiting to accept you for who you are. Rainbows! Unicorns! Yes!

Plus, once you meet other queer kids and adults, you'll discover that we've got a whole bunch of things that are unique to us, like drag shows, lesbian music festivals, softball tournaments, pride marches, and even our own slang. There's an entire queer history that you can claim as your own, and your individual flair and smarts will help that history grow.

PINGING YOUR PEOPLE

So where are you going to find your new queer best friend? You can't just call 1-800-GAY-BFFS. You'll have to look around a bit to find other queer kids to hang out with. But don't worry; it's not that hard. Here are some ideas.

⊚ **Locate queer meeting places.** If you live in a city, you may be in luck. Most big cities—and even some smaller ones—now have some kind of queer community center. The Trevor Project (see Resources section) has a resource guide to help you locate queer services near your home. You can also just type "gay," "queer," or "LGBT" along with "teen" or "youth" and your city name into a search engine and see if anything comes up. Finding a group for trans teens can be harder, but some centers have specific meetings for trans and genderqueer folks. Even if there's not a specific trans group, trans youth are, of course, welcome at queer centers.

⊚ **Access queer youth chat rooms.** If you live in a smaller town, it may be more difficult to find local kids, but you can always go online to meet people. In gay youth chat rooms and forums, you can meet other queer kids from all over the world (and maybe some from your town as well). It's best to keep your identity vague and not to dole out personal information when first talking in chat rooms because you don't know who is on the other end of the chat. And be careful about what you click on after doing a search. You may enter "gay youth" to find other gay peers in your neighborhood, but your search engine might interpret that as "gay youth porn." It's unfortunate but true. If the site has a bad vibe, leave it and try a different one.

◎ **Join a Gay-Straight Alliance.** Gay-Straight Alliances (GSAs) are popping up in more and more schools. They're clubs for queer kids and their allies to meet, organize, educate each other, and have fun together. If your school has a GSA, that's the logical place to meet other like-minded teens. If your school doesn't have a group and another local school does, see if you can attend meetings there. Use your connections and ask around about other queer teens in your vicinity, if you feel comfortable. If you're out to your friends, ask them if they know someone they can introduce you to.

◎ **Find other like-minded groups.** If you find yourself in a place where there really aren't many LGBT teens and you aren't sure if your current friends will be accepting, there are some places where you're likely to meet straight kids who'll have your back. See if there are any progressive teen groups in your area that emphasize acceptance and outreach to people who are different. Organizations like Planned Parenthood (plannedparenthood.org) and AIDS resource centers often have youth groups that are not specifically for LGBT teens, but would be open to having you join them.

◎ **Use your gaydar.** Since it's estimated that approximately 10 percent of all people are LGBT, it's pretty likely that there are other LGBT teens in your school. You've just got to hone your gaydar and see if you can figure out who they are. He may be in the lane next to you at track practice or playing the trumpet in the school band. She may be that shy freshman who's obsessed with rap music. And like we said, some stereotypes are true: There's probably a gay boy (who loves Beyoncé) in the drama club and a lesbian or bi girl (with a wallet chain and spiky hair) on the softball team. If you think certain kids are LGBT, figure out a way to get friendly with them. You can drop hints that you're queer or prod a little to see if they'll come out to you. Once you make one LGBT friend, you'll soon be on your way to forming your own queer posse.

Stepping Outside the Pink Triangle

Once you find some queer friends and start living your proud LGBT life it can be easy to get trapped in the "pink triangle," where you reject anything that doesn't conform to your queer politics and expectations. You might start looking down on straight people because you think they just don't get it or isolating yourself from the larger world because you only feel safe around other queers. Naturally, you're excited about your identity and want to explore it. But don't let that get in the way of all the non-queer-specific opportunities that life has to offer! Your sexual identity is just one part of the bigger picture.

In the end, your best friends may not be other queer kids, but hetero hipsters, hippies, jocks, goths, nerds, or just the kids next door. The fact that you're queer doesn't mean that all straight people are nightmares! (Believe us, you'll find out that other queer people aren't always the winners of Miss Congeniality.) Having straight friends (of both genders) is important, even if they do sometimes ask annoying questions about your sex life or don't always understand the sting of homophobia. *Fag hags* (straight girls who hang out with gay guys) and *lezbros* (straight guys who befriend lesbians) make great support, and you'll never have to worry about losing those friendships due to romantic complications!

How I Found the Lesbians

When I got to college, I was finally out and wanted to meet other LGBT students, so I did the logical thing: I joined the gay and lesbian student union. I met some really great people, but there was one problem: 99 percent of them were guys. They were all very nice, but I really wanted to meet some girls.

One day on campus I saw a sign for a folk music concert. I don't know why, but something about the woman's photo made me think "lesbian." I gathered my courage and dragged my room-mate to the show in a small room in the student union. I don't remember anything about the musician or the songs she sang. All I focused on were the two women sitting in front of me holding hands throughout the show. After the concert, a girl who lived in my dorm approached me and invited me to come to a feminist film the next week, sponsored by the college women's center, the same group that hosted the concert. It was there that I discovered that many of the lesbians on campus were more involved with feminist issues than with the gay student union—most of the women in the women's center were lesbian or bisexual! Finally, I found my girls!

I quickly became involved in the group, organizing feminist film showings, a radio program, and a lecture series. I stayed involved with the gay and lesbian student union, too, dragging my new friends to their events and getting the union to host more events that would appeal to women. By the time I graduated, the union was about 40 percent women and also had a few trans members. Not only did I find my people, I also helped to bring these two groups together!

FINDING ADULT ALLIES

There's usually one teacher who everyone thinks is cool. You'll know who it is because, on any given weekday, you'll find a whole bunch of students hanging out in his or her classroom after school, discussing the pros and cons of vegetarianism or debating presidential politics.

If you're not sure if a teacher or faculty member is supportive, you can suss them out, much like you would a fellow student. Does she prohibit homophobic jokes in her classroom? Does anyone who uses the word faggot get reprimanded? Is there a "safe zone" sticker with a pink triangle on her bulletin board? If so, chances are this teacher is one you can trust.

Another great place to find adult allies is PFLAG, Parents, Families, and Friends of Lesbians and Gays (pflag.org). If there's a meeting in your area, check it out. If you're getting any grief from your family about being gay, PFLAG is awesome about giving you some hope.

Don't overlook that supportive uncle, neighbor, or librarian. The lesbian couple down the block, the trans guy who fixes your dad's car, or your mom's gay hairdresser might want to take you under their wings. Or hell, even your parents could be your greatest allies.

KNOW YOUR RIGHTS

Part of navigating your queer sphere is to know—
legally—what your rights are. You can start by
checking out the American Civil Liberties Union
(aclu.org), which is a national organization that has
fought for a lot of LGBT teens' rights. If you go to a
public school, your rights in school are the same as
they are out of school. If you go to a private school,
you don't have the same rights as kids in public school.
That's because public schools are considered part of the
government and are protected by the US Constitution,
whereas private schools are governed by something
called contract law. Often private schools have a code
of conduct that is outlined in their student handbooks.

Here are answers to some common questions about
school. These responses are based upon government
laws, so again, if you go to a private school, you'll have
to check in with your student handbook to see your
particular school's policies.

Q: Can I wear a gay rights T-shirt to school?
A: Generally, your right to express your opinion
is protected under the First Amendment of the US
Constitution. That means you should be free to express
your opinion as long as it doesn't disrupt the learning environment. You might be banned from wearing
a sexually explicit T-shirt or a revealing outfit because
those are considered disruptive. It also depends upon
the school's rules about T-shirts. But the school has to
treat all students the same. For example, if the school lets
someone wear a T-shirt proclaiming a political view or

social belief, it should allow you to express yours. But if your school has a rule against such T-shirts, then no, you won't be allowed to wear a gay slogan T-shirt to school.

And remember: Not all proqueer slogans are the same. Your school may consider "Equality Now!" to be OK. But that doesn't mean that they'll necessarily like it if you wear a T-shirt that says "Same-Sex Marriage is Sexy!" or "Straight People Are Sooo Gay!" You may be able to wear something saying "I Like Girls" but not "Your Girlfriend Wants Me." It can be tricky. It's also good to question your motives when wearing something that is thought to be political. Are you making a case? Or just vying for attention? Sometimes it's a little bit of both, but getting your queer butt sent home from school for your "inappropriate clothing" won't help other queer kids' views to be taken seriously.

Q: Can I bring a same-sex date to prom?
A: The good news is that LGBT students have made a lot of progress in recent years with the right to bring a same-sex date to the prom. The not-so-good news is that if you live in a conservative area, your school may say that it doesn't allow it. Still, the right to bring a same-sex date to the prom or other school function is considered a form of free expression, so you should absolutely fight for it. Students in recent years have won the right in court to bring same-sex dates to the prom. If your school is telling you that you can't or kicks you out when you do, contact the ACLU for help.

Q: What if I'm being bullied at school?
A: If you are being harassed at school and you report it, your school has the responsibility to do something about it. If you are being harassed for being LGBT, report it to a principal or counselor. Make sure to keep your own notes about what is happening to you, when you reported it, and to whom. If things don't get better, get your parents involved. However, your school should not out you to your parents without your permission. Nor should they allow teachers or staff to make antigay remarks about you or punish you for holding hands with a same-sex partner if they allow opposite sex couples to do the same. For more on how to respond if someone is harassing you, see Chapter 4.

Q: What if I want to identify as another gender at school?
A: Unfortunately, this is a complex legal question that hasn't been tested much in courts. So it may depend on how far you want to go and what type of school you attend. If you wish to be called "he" instead of "she" and perhaps take on a different name, some of your teachers may be supportive, realizing that it may make you more comfortable in an academic atmosphere. But if you're a boy who prefers to dress like a girl or vice versa, then you may be violating school dress codes. And if you wish to use the public bathroom of your new gender, it's possible that someone will protest. If it becomes an issue, your parents may need to get involved and work with you and your school to come to an agreement. If that's not something you can ask them

to do, you may need to wait until high school is over to be able to fully express yourself. You can also contact the ACLU with any questions about your rights.

ON THE QUEER FRONTIER

1955

LESBIAN LIFE, LOVE, AND LITERATURE

The lesbian community wasn't always an easy thing to find. In the 1950s, there were no lesbian online communities, magazines, bookstores, dating services, or film festivals. There were gay and lesbian bars, but those were vulnerable to police raids, and some women didn't want to be in bars around drinking. So in 1955, San Francisco lesbian couple Del Martin and Phyllis Lyon, along with three other lesbian couples, decided to start the social group Daughters of Bilitis (DOB)—named after an 1894 collection of erotic poetry called *The Songs of Bilitis*—which had discussion groups, social events, and activism initiatives. Soon there were DOB chapters in New York, Chicago, Los Angeles, Philadelphia, and Washington, DC, and most joined efforts with local gay male groups like the Mattachine Society. Soon the DOB started a literary and news magazine called *The Ladder*, which became a lifeline to lesbians countrywide. Most chapters have since folded, but the organization gave way to more modern groups like Gay Liberation Front and Lesbian Nation, and *The Ladder* was inspiration for later lesbian mags like *Curve* and *Go*.

How Marke Found His Posse

When I came out, I wanted to find my people. But I was different from a lot of the gay guys I knew. I didn't like the same music they did or the same types of fashion. None of the other gay guys read a lot of books, and I was a total bookworm. I thought that because we didn't have a lot in common, I could never be friends with them. But closing myself off made me look like a big snob. I really needed to connect with other gay people. How else would I ever get a date, right? So I took a giant social leap and befriended the gayest-acting guy in school—the one who wore expensive preppy clothes and who everyone had nicknamed "Swish." (Really, that's what they called him.)

I thought we'd have nothing in common. I was completely wrong. Sure, I wasn't into his collection of designer colognes, and he wasn't much interested in my favorite punk bands and Japanese novels. But we actually had a lot in common—and not just the whole queer thing. He loved dancing as much as I did and took me out to my first all-ages club, introducing me to the "gay corner" of the dance floor. We also both adored modern art, and he invited me to the museum downtown with some gay art lovers from other schools. I even got him to mosh with me to Minor Threat and the Sex Pistols in the school cafeteria.

I met an entire network of other queer kids through Swish, and I'm still friends with most of them to this day. Finally, I could relax and be myself around other LGBT people. I'm really glad I took a chance on someone who didn't seem like me at all. (Otherwise, I'd probably still be reading Jane Austen in my parents' basement.)

GET INVOLVED!

One of the best ways to feel part of the queer community and simultaneously to feel good about yourself is to get involved in making a difference for other LGBTs in the world. Participating in community-building activities will look great on your college application, and who knows: It may just snag you a boyfriend or girlfriend, too! Getting involved helps to build your character and to give you extra confidence — two total turn-ons. Here are some ways to take part in queer life.

◉ **Plan for the National Day of Silence.** Every year, students from hundreds of schools from around the country take a vow of silence for one day to draw attention to all the LGBT youth who are silenced by antigay harassment and violence. It started in 1996 with more than 150 students at the University of Virginia. A year later, 100 schools joined in, and now hundreds of thousands of students from more than 8,000 schools and universities participate. It typically takes place in April, and it's a great way to show your solidarity with the LGBT community. Lately many schools and teens have launched super creative web campaigns, design projects, and viral videos to spread the word. To find out what's going on in your area, visit dayofsilence.org.

◉ **Join your local LGBT community center.** This is a great way to meet other teens from different schools, find out what's going on in the greater LGBT community, and learn a bit about LGBT culture and history. Center Link is a national organization for LGBT community centers, and its website (see Resources section) can connect you to one in your area. At your local center you can give support and peer counseling to other kids who are coming out and get involved with art, writing, theater, and political groups. You can volunteer to help older or less fortunate LGBT people in the community or join an outreach program to speak in schools and the community about LGBT issues.

◎ **Join or start a Gay-Straight Alliance.** Even if you don't think you need one, having a GSA in your school makes it safer for other LGBT kids. A study by the Gay, Lesbian, and Straight Education Network (GLSEN) found that in schools with GSAs, students heard fewer homophobic remarks and experienced less harassment and assault because of sexual orientation or gender identity. If students were harassed, they were more likely to report it. In general, LGBT students felt more secure in schools with a GSA. Plus, having a GSA is really fun and a great way to make queer friends. The GSA Network (gsanetwork.org) has some great info about how to start and maintain a kick-ass GSA at your school.

◎ **Volunteer for political campaigns.** While being LGBT is not a political decision, gaining rights as a queer person is. So getting involved in politics is a good way to ensure that your own rights are protected. Even if you can't vote yet, you can help inform your community about important issues or

candidates who have philosophies you believe in. Perhaps there is a great candidate running for office who is promoting gay marriage rights; you can support him or her. Or maybe there is an antigay ballot initiative in your town or a group working for trans-employment rights. Join in the fight! Getting involved in political campaigns when you're young teaches you valuable communication skills, helps you make contacts in your community, and gives you a hands-on opportunity to learn how the system works.

◎ **Launch or join an online community.** You probably have your own blog or Facebook page. Why not use it to spread the word about causes and issues you feel passionate about, either by joining online groups and contributing to the discussion or by starting your own groups and fan pages? If you're extra tech savvy, you can register your own domain and start a forum that addresses specific things you feel strongly about. It's a sad thing, but young and strong LGBT voices are often missing from debates. Other people, both LGBT and straight, really do want to know what you think. Use your cyber voice to speak out! Be sure to follow internet etiquette while online. If you disrespect or insult people, your opinion likely won't be heard or taken seriously. Focus on the issue and not on the person speaking. Never use obscene, abusive, or sexually explicit language. You're unlikely to change the opinion of an angry bigot, but your thoughtful counter-argument may sway someone else viewing the page who is undecided on a particular issue.

START YOUR OWN REVOLUTION

Some of the best ideas for making change can come from you. Maybe you and your friends have been complaining about an issue in your community that really pisses you off. Take those feelings of anger and frustration and put them to work. Start your own day of observance, hold a car wash fundraiser to support an LGBT rights organization, or start your own LGBT rights organization. We're sure you can come up with a hundred creative ways to make your voice heard, make your point, and maybe even make some big changes in the world.

You don't have to be a big political activist either to make a difference. Just speaking up about your experiences to people who don't understand or befriending a lonely queer kid can make all the difference in the world.

FIND A GREAT QUEER COLLEGE

If you're going away to college, you'll want to research schools where you'll be comfortable as a queer person so you can focus on your studies while enjoying a robust campus life. Most colleges in major metropolitan areas will be somewhat gay friendly, and some small colleges in small towns can also be magnets for queer academics. But you'll have to vet them all first to see if they're right for you. How should you start your selection process?

First, narrow your colleges down to ones that offer what you want to study (assuming you know what you want to study). You could go to the most gay-friendly school in the planet, but if it doesn't offer your dream dual-major of musical theater and astrophysics, then

ON THE QUEER FRONTIER   1952

THE FIRST LADY OF NEW YORK

Professional nightclub and stage performer Christine Jorgensen did a lot more than just entertain audiences. Born George William Jorgensen Jr., Christine became famous in 1952 as one of the first well-known sex-change recipients. An American, she traveled to Denmark where she had to undergo years of surgery and hormone therapy to become a woman. The entire world was fascinated by her transformation, and the smoky-voiced blonde became an instant celebrity. Jorgensen granted a few, select interviews about her journey from male to female, but was more interested in turning the public's attention toward her new career as an entertainer and performer. She appeared on stages and at dozens of college campuses and later appeared in theaters to sold-out crowds in New York City and Las Vegas.

what's the point? Once you've found a place that offers what you want to study, get online and dig deeper. Check out the school's nondiscrimination policy. Does it include sexual orientation? Gender identity? See if there are any classes in queer studies. Does the university have a Gay-Straight Alliance or other gay student organization? Check out the Princeton Review of Colleges, which each year ranks the most and least gay-friendly colleges.

Once you've narrowed it down to the schools that interest you, call and request a catalogue and list of courses. Read the campus paper on the web to see what makes the news and read the editorials and letters to the editor to see if campus dialogue gels with your beliefs. Make a list of the things you want to find out about the school. Finally, go to the school—if you can—and check it out yourself. In addition to investigating the course of study you want to pursue, keep an eye out for any signs of gay life on campus.

While you're on your campus tour, use your gaydar. Are there any openly LGBT couples walking to class? Are there gay flyers on the bulletin boards? Get in touch with someone at the LGBT campus organization (call or email) and see if you can meet up with someone while you're on campus. Hearing from other LGBT students can help you get a true picture of what the actual campus climate is like.

Also, see if your college offers gender-neutral housing. Colleges traditionally required people of the same sex to live together in dorms, but more and more colleges are recognizing that, regardless of one's sexual orientation, sometimes people choose to live with someone of a different gender. For trans kids, a policy like this might be essential in choosing where to go to school.

Trouble in Paradise

We throw the term LGBT around like we're all one big happy family. And for the most part, we are. But like any family, not everyone always gets along. There are times when some lesbians don't want gay men around because they believe them to be sexist, and gay men sometimes reject lesbians in their social circles because they think it threatens their tight-knit male community. Some lesbians and gay men give bisexuals a hard time because they want them to "choose" one or the other. And trans people sometimes feel left out of the queer community altogether because the trans community is only just starting to come into its own. In fact, a lot of ignorance and misconceptions remain—even among other queer people—about what it means to be trans. The important thing to realize is that this kind of petty divisiveness between queer peeps only hurts the community as a whole. If you feel like your queer brothers and sisters are giving you unnecessary grief, remind them to love thy fellow queer. At the end of the day, being queer is about acceptance and diversity. Our symbol is a rainbow, after all!

FOUR

RISING ABOVE

HOW TO OVERCOME QUEERPHOBIA

You're queer.

We think that's awesome. Your boyfriend or girlfriend does, too. Maybe your mom, your whole school, and even Ellen DeGeneres are working on a snappy surprise musical number about what a fine out-and-proud member of the community you are. Somebody call in the marching band! Toot the trumpets and twirl those sparkly batons!

We love that you fly a rainbow flag on your desk, wear hot pink scarves to school, or set your profile to "interested in men and women." Seriously. By celebrating your life and feeling comfortable about who you are, you're setting an exciting example—and maybe making life a little easier—for kids still trapped in the closet.

Chances are, though, there's someone out there who, for whatever reason, is totally bugged out by the fact that you're LGBT. It may be someone you're close to, like your dad or your cousin, or it may be some random idiot that really needs to get a life and stop paying so much attention to yours. At some point, unfortunately, you're going to encounter haters.

Maybe you've been stalked by thugs at the mall who yell homophobic insults, or your boss has made you feel uncomfortable by constantly joking about your sexuality, or your uncle has tried to shame the gay out of you.

Or maybe you've been called names by your classmates, shoved against the lockers as someone walks past you, bullied online, or even called a "he-she" by your teacher—and not one person in charge has done jack about it. Well, you're not alone. The Gay, Lesbian, Straight Education Network (GLSEN) found that, in 2007, 86 percent of LGBT teens were verbally harassed at school, 44 percent reported being physically harassed, and 22 percent said they had been physically assaulted because of their sexual orientation.

Remember that some of the world's most exciting artists, scientists, and thinkers had to triumph over some kind of harassment or hardship as a kid. It doesn't feel good now, but you will survive. And as you climb your way to fabulousness, you'll be able to look back at all of the small-minded people who got on your case and thank them for teaching you exactly what kind of person you want to be (someone unlike them). Until then, keep your head high and learn how to protect yourself—without sinking to their level.

WHY DO PEOPLE HATE?

If you're getting grief from someone at school or elsewhere, it can be hard to wrap your brain around why. You've done nothing wrong to anyone, but people seem set on making your life hell. Even though it feels like there isn't much you can do about some people's bad attitudes, it does help to understand why they have them.

ON THE QUEER FRONTIER   1977

VOTE FOR HARVEY MILK!

If you've seen the movie *Milk*, you know all about Harvey Milk. He moved from his home state of New York to San Francisco in 1972 and opened a camera shop on Castro Street in the heart of San Francisco's up-and-coming gay neighborhood, the Castro. Milk then became interested in politics and, after years of campaigning and losing multiple elections, he secured a seat on the San Francisco Board of Supervisors in 1977. The first openly homosexual politician to get elected in the city's history, Milk was responsible for getting the city to pass one of the country's first bills to protect queer rights. Sadly, he was assassinated in 1978 after only 11 months in office by a fellow board member, Dan White, who was judged to be temporarily insane. Always an optimistic thinker, Milk coined the expression, "You gotta give 'em hope."

One reason that people are cruel to others is because they are afraid of what they don't know. If they've never met a queer person before, they might feel intimidated by you. It's odd but true. And some kids are simply taught to hate or distrust what they don't know or understand. In other situations, peer pressure comes into play, and people go along with awful things because they need to feel accepted. It's also important to remember that lots of bigots are full of insecurity, and insecure people will take out their own anxieties about themselves on others—especially on kids who are in a minority, like LGBT kids. When you don't feel good about yourself, it's tempting to hate on someone else to try to make yourself feel better, and a queer kid in drama class is an easier target than the straight captain of the football team. While understanding all of this doesn't make it any easier when you're getting abused by someone, it can help you to take it less personally. It's not about you—it's about them.

TRIUMPHING OVER HATERS

So someone in your life is on your case for absolutely no reason. What should you do? Even if you're a strong person with love and support at home and an awesome group of friends, being harassed about your sexual orientation can be demoralizing and exhausting. And if you don't have that support at home, it can feel even worse. If you're being harassed for being queer you can (and should!) fight back. Here are some ways to do that without resorting to violence.

◎ **Stand up for yourself.** Tell the people harping on you that they're only being immature and that nothing is going to change you, so they should find someone else to pick on. Try not to escalate the situation. If someone raises his or her voice, just walk away. You've said what you had to say. Let them entertain themselves some other way.

◎ **Tell someone.** If there are supportive adults in your life, let them know what's going on. You're not a wimp or a tattle-tale if you tell someone about the harassment you're forced to endure. And you don't have to mention that you're being taunted for being queer if you don't want to. Most schools have strong policies against bullying, and they don't care why you're being harassed, just that you are. Having said that, if you are OK being out, it's good to tell a supervisor at your school that you're being targeted because you're queer. That way, they can do something about it on a larger scale and help other LGBT kids who are in a similar situation.

◎ **Stick with friends.** Bullies are cowards. They're less likely to mess with you if you're with a friend or, even better, an entire posse of your friends. So if you're going to be in a situation that you know is vulnerable, bring a couple of sidekicks along.

DEALING WITH PHYSICAL
OR SEXUAL ASSAULT

Unfortunately, LGBT people are still the victims of hate crimes, which means they are physically attacked or sexually assaulted because of their sexual orientation or gender identity. According to the FBI, sexual orientation or gender identity is the third most likely reason, after race and religion, for bias-related attacks.

It's hard to know what to do when you're attacked. In some cases, the best thing to do is to run, yell, or fight back. In other situations, you might feel like the thing that will keep you safest is to not resist. Follow your instincts and trust that you did the best you could to protect yourself. And remember that no matter where or when you were attacked, it was not your fault.

As soon as you can, get to a safe place. Talk to someone you trust. Get an adult involved. Report what happened to the police. If you were sexually assaulted, don't change your clothes or take a shower. You may feel like the first thing you want to do is to get clean, but the police may need evidence. If antigay slurs were used against you, report that. You don't have to say whether you are gay or not.

Get support from a rape crisis hotline or the Trevor help line (thetrevorproject.org), a 24-hour crisis and counseling center specifically for young queer people.

WHEN DEMOCRACY FEELS LIKE HYPOCRISY

Imagine you're sitting there in English class, trying to stay awake, when the teacher assigns a position paper on the topic "Should Same-Sex Marriage Be Legal?" Oh great. That means some of your classmates are going to start researching and arguing why you shouldn't have the same rights. Great way to start out a Monday, eh?

The way the political climate is right now, a lot of gay issues like marriage are being debated in very public forums, like over the airwaves and internet, at the ballot box, and in highly publicized court cases. Both of us have voted on things like gay marriage in our own states. We've won some fights, and we've lost others. And even though we think it's a shame that equal rights is something that people need to vote on, we know that we need to stand up for our rights, so we vote.

But it's often easy to feel like you're under attack. You may have to listen to politicians tell lies about you, watch hateful and misleading commercials, and even hear people you know and love say they're going to vote against you. You might feel like you don't know where you stand with people in your life. You can get paranoid, wondering if the guy behind the counter selling you that sandwich is pro or antigay. It is degrading and can really wear on your self-esteem.

We've both found that the best way to feel good about ourselves in situations like this is to throw ourselves into the fight for the cause. Unfortunately, you might not be able to vote yet, but there is stuff you can do. Write editorials for the school paper and letters to the editor of your local paper. Volunteer for the campaign. Organize students at your school to get involved. Have a bake sale or a dance to raise money to support the cause or a candidate who's supportive. And always try to stay positive and make good connections with people — both queer and straight — who are on your side. In the end, if your campaign loses, remember that it's just one battle. Real change often takes a few tries. So don't give up hope. Instead, know that you did everything you could to stand up for what you believe. And the next time the issue is up for a vote, jump back in again and go for the win.

Kathy and the Homophobic Park Incident

In 2006, people in Oregon were asked to vote on a constitutional amendment to ban same-sex marriage. I was doing all I could to fight for our rights. I volunteered for my local gay rights organization, canvassed door to door, and put a pro–gay marriage sign on my lawn and bumper sticker on my car.

One Saturday, my partner and I took our dogs to the neighborhood park. When we returned to the car, I found a note on the windshield that said, "Gays go home. This is a straight park!" I was shocked and scared. It was one of our favorite places to bring the dogs, and suddenly I felt unsafe.

My partner and I drove home in silence, upset and not sure what to say. When we got home, I burst into tears. The culmination of weeks of TV and radio ads, "One Man, One Woman" bumper stickers, and neighbors with "Protect Marriage" lawn signs had gotten to me. We decided to call the police and file a report about the note. Even if they never caught the people, we felt it was important that the threat be documented.

After the officer left, my neighbor, a straight woman whom I considered to be a good friend, came over to see why the police were at our house. I could see her hiding a smirk as I told the story. Finally she burst out laughing and told me that she was the one who put the note on my car. She thought it was funny. A joke. I looked at her, incredulous. I considered her a friend and ally, but I knew she could never understand how under siege I felt as a queer person in that kind of political climate. She apologized and also tried to console me when we lost the election. I still love her dearly, but the incident did make me realize that it's really hard for most of the world to understand what it is like to walk through life as a queer person.

OH, GOD—YOU'RE GAY

Somehow, God always comes into the picture when queer people come out. No matter whether you're a devout Christian or a nonbeliever, you can be sure that someone somewhere is going to tell you what God thinks about your being queer. (As if they even knew.)

God-against-gays people typically fall into one of three categories:

- ◉ **The "God hates fags" people.** These people use religion to justify their ignorant viewpoints and tell you that you're going to burn in hell for being gay.

- ◉ **The "God can help you" people.** These people try to convince you that God will help you become straight. They will try to "save" you in this way. And they are big fans of reparative therapy (see page 55).

- ◉ **The "hate the sin, love the sinner" people.** These people try to tell you that, even if you can't help being gay, you should never act on it because gay sex is immoral and ungodly.

We're not religious scholars, but we do know there is a lot of debate happening within churches and religious organizations right now about the place of LGBT people in the eyes of God. If you are religious, we encourage you to investigate your own faith and come to your own conclusions.

What do you do when you run into someone who has a religious viewpoint that is opposed to homosexuality? The answer depends on how much you care. For instance, if it's a religious viewpoint that you are not in any way connected to, it can be easy enough to agree to disagree or to ignore the zealot's proselytizing. But what if you are Christian and your church teaches that homosexuality is a sin? How can you resolve your own beliefs with the teachings of your church?

You may want to find a new place of worship. There are people within your faith—be it Christian, Muslim, Jewish, Hindu, Mormon, Buddhist, or whatever—who believe that God loves everyone, including your homo-licious self! Lots of congregations are now accepting queer people into the fold, and you just need to find the right one for you. (See the Resources section to find out how to connect with queer-friendly religious leaders and institutions in your area.)

Because of the confines some of established religions, many LGBT people establish their own brand of spirituality, independent of organized religion, or even work within specific religious traditions. You're free to believe in whatever kind of God you like and to worship—or not worship—as you choose.

BAITING AND SOCIAL TRAPS

Some teens (and even some adults) who aren't as mentally mature as you are may think that being queer is a big joke, or that playing tricks on you because you're LGBT is hilarious. In fact, a recent study reported that 54 percent of LGBT teens have been cyber-bullied by having humiliating photos of them posted online, rumors spread about them, or cruel online polls created about them. Other kids may try to use your queerness to punk you. For example, they might pose as someone else online and arrange to meet you somewhere, only to arrive with a group of their friends to "prove" that you're gay. They may lead you on with a string of flirty IMs and texts that they're really laughing about with their friends. They may invite you to a party just to make fun of you. Or in a more serious situation, they may lure you somewhere alone with the promise of friendship or confidentiality and then jump you with a bunch of other thugs.

We're not trying to scare the hot pants off you, and you shouldn't be paranoid about making new friends. Sometimes the head cheerleader really does have a crush on you and wants to meet you in secret, or maybe that funny guy in your science class actually feels like he needs to confide in you about his conflicted emotions or same-sex attractions. But you should be careful.

Here are some queer-safe rules to live by.

◉ If you're going to go out with someone you've never been out with before, tell a friend where you're going and see if you can check in with him or her in an hour or so to make sure it's all cool.

◉ Keep your cell handy when going to meet someone you don't know well, just in case you need to make a rescue call.

◉ Always carry money on you (keep it somewhere hidden, like your sock) so you can grab a bus or taxi if you need to get out of somewhere.

◉ Approach any new flirts with a measure of caution, and don't say anything that you could later be embarrassed by until you're sure that person's for real.

◉ If you get invited to a party by people you don't know, ask if you can bring your friends along for backup.

◉ If someone is harassing you online, change your profile to private, block his or her address, and refuse to respond.

There's no way to avoid being embarrassed by jokers in high school; it happens to everyone who's a little different, whether because of their weight, intelligence, sexual orientation, or whatever. Just be true to yourself and act with dignity. If you blow it off and rise above it, you'll be the one laughing in the end.

RELAX, REBOOT, RECENTER

Being a teen comes with a lot of pressure. Being a queer teen comes with even more. You may get really frustrated and angry sometimes. Those are valid feelings, and it's OK to have them. But you don't need to act on them. Try to avoid plotting revenge scenarios or getting obsessed about what others think of you. Revenge plots can seriously backfire, and obsessions just suck away all of your energy. Channel your negative emotions instead into creative projects or planning your future. Soon you'll be able to get the hell out and never see any of these nutcases again. Revenge will be yours when you win your Academy Award or Nobel Peace Prize or just wind up in a healthier, more meaningful relationship than all of these people could ever attain.

It takes a lot of strength to be brave and live your life and even more to not become a hater yourself. But remember that hating takes a lot of energy and puts negativity into the world, so save your energy for things that will better yourself and promote understanding. When you feel that the pressures are getting to be too much or that no one will ever understand you, step back, take a deep breath, and get some perspective on the situation. Try to relax. Go somewhere you feel safe or comfortable to reboot and start again. Keep a hold of your inner self. Listen to some favorite music. Talk to someone who understands. Write a poem. If you find your mind is spinning off in too

IN MARKE'S WORDS

On the Wrong Team

When I was a freshman, I was briefly on the track team. I was excited because our track coach was also my English teacher, and English was my favorite class. OK, I also had a bit of a crush on him. He was cute!

Things were going great until one day, out of the blue, he called me off the track and told me to run in place in front of everyone else. As I was running, he started laughing and said, "You run like a faggot!" That made everyone else laugh at me, too. You can bet I ran out of there (like a faggot) and found an empty room in the school to cry. I was mortified.

When I told my school counselor and my vice principal, I didn't get very much support. The counselor told me that gay people weren't very good at sports anyway, and I should try a different hobby, like hairdressing. (What?) And my vice principal took the opportunity to tell me that I should wear nicer clothes. (As if that had anything to do with anything.) My parents weren't much help, either; they basically said to just try to move on, but I was too upset to hear that.

A couple of days later, this popular guy Chris came up to me at my locker and said he had heard about what happened. I thought he was going to laugh at me, too. But instead he told me he was putting together an intramural basketball team and wanted to know if I'd like to join. At first I thought it might be a trap, so I just told him I'd come to one of the practices and see. After all, there's a lot of running in basketball, and I didn't want live through another bad experience. But it turned out he actually thought I was a good athlete and really did want me for the team. I made some great friends on that team, and was glad to find out that there were cool people in the world to balance out the jerks.

many directions, try meditating, exercising, dancing, or anything that brings you back into your body and helps you to get a clearer vision of the amazing person you are and your goals for the future. It's easy to feel sorry for yourself, but that doesn't move you ahead; it only holds you back. Do what it takes to stay on a positive path, even if that means ignoring a lot of the bull happening around you. Often, better times are just around the corner.

FIVE

MAKING YOUR MOVE

QUEER DATING

So you think coming out and dealing with haters is hard? Try dating! No, just kidding. Dating is, of course, one of best parts about being queer. But it does mean taking a risk and making a little bit of effort. Mr. Wonderful probably isn't going to just gallop up to your castle, fight his way past the flying monkeys to the throne room, and plop himself down in your royal lap. And Ms. Right may not be waiting for you at your locker in her hot soccer short-shorts with a pair of front-row tickets to the rest of your amazing life together. But does that mean you should resign yourself to a lonely life of lying around in your fuzzy Big Bird slippers with your 23 cats, eating bowl after bowl of chicken noodle soup while you secretly wonder what might have been? Hardly. You're just going to have to put yourself out there.

Dating can often be awkward and stressful no matter your age, sexual orientation, or however laidback you try to be about it. But as a queer teen, you've got a few more challenges on your plate. For one, your options are limited: There may not be many other available queer teens around to practice your skills on, let alone ones you find attractive. On top of that, your parents might not be comfortable with the idea or could even actively discourage you from dating someone of your own gender. And there isn't exactly an overload of examples of wonderful queer dating in the media or in history class. You're breaking new ground every time you ask someone out. Sometimes this can lead to frustration, like trying to fit size-13 feet into a dainty pair of Cinderella glass pumps.

Even us fairy godmothers still have our share of crazy meet-ups. Marke once took a guy on a date to a play — and the guy actually brought his grandmother with him! Not only that, but he also expected Marke to buy all three tickets and then did nothing but complain, loudly, all the way through. Needless to say, there was no second date (even though Marke totally bonded with Grandma over how rude her grandkid was).

So relax. You're just starting to explore your romantic options. A fantastic world of possibilities is peeking out, not like some unfortunate girl's G-string but like the hot-pink sun at the dawn of a new, potentially awesome day. This is the fun part, and it's not as hard as you may think it is. You can use the whole dating thing to gain confidence while learning more about yourself and the world around you. And remember these words from a wise old drag queen: "Those who don't go for it never know from it!"

IS YOUR CRUSH ON THE SAME TEAM?

OK, there's this really cute girl in your Gay-Straight Alliance who makes your heart vibrate louder than your phone every time she texts you. Or maybe there's an amazing guy in your science class, and you're wondering if there's any real chemistry between you. Should you start flirting?

Here's where things get tricky. To lessen your chances of rejection, find out if your crush plays on the lavender team. How do you figure out if someone is LGBT or not without coming off like a total dork or a stalker? You just need to be sly. Here's a hypothetical situation.

Sasha's in your Spanish class. You just love the way that wisp of black hair falls in front of her eye. Plus she cracks you up big time. You always save seats for each other and research swear words in foreign languages to share with each other. You're becoming good friends, but you start to feel something deeper and want to ask her out on an official date. Would she be down?

First, figure out how she feels about gay or trans people in general. If the topic has never come up, drop it into conversation, like suggesting you two research the word gay in another language and see if she melts into a pile of annoying giggles or honestly seems interested in pursuing the topic. You could talk about famous people who've dressed in drag for movies, TV shows, or photo shoots. Or you could ask her what teachers she thinks are cute and then tell her you've got the hots for Ms. Peltier, the health teacher. Or, hey, why not go for broke and just flat out ask her if she'd ever kiss a girl? (In Spanish, of course. It will sound way cooler.)

Once you've brought up the topic, assess her reaction and decide whether or not to proceed. If she says she likes girls, too, great news. If she likes both boys and girls, then she may be open to dating bi or trans people (more about trans dating on page 103). But if she says she's straight, set your sights elsewhere. You can no more make a straight girl gay than she could make you want to be with boys. (The same obviously goes for straight guys.)

Of course, some LGBT kids take longer to come out than others, and it may take them awhile to admit it to you. If you sense that's the case, be patient. It's best not to push and to let people come out at their own pace.

INVESTIGATING FURTHER

Maybe you're still not sure if your crush is queer—or if you even like him or her in that way. Love doesn't always happen at first sight, and when it does, it doesn't always last. If you're on the fence, work on getting to know your love interest better.

If he's a schoolmate, make a point to get to know him outside of the academic setting. You don't want every conversation to be about the difficulty of the algebra test or why your lockers were built in the Stone Age and are always stuck shut. That won't get you anywhere but Boringsville. Besides, school is a world of its own. You need to observe him in a different setting to see if you really gel. Find an excuse to hang out after school: watch a soccer game, grab a burrito, go shopping. Friendship is a great precursor to dating. And sometimes—like after watching him shove fries up his nose and pretend to be a walrus—you may decide that friendship is the best way to go after all.

If you feel ready, you can come out to him. If he's queer, he'll probably tell you. If you're getting confusing messages, you might have to ask flat out. "Would you ever date a guy?" If he says he would, woo hoo! You're on your way. If not and you like him enough as a person, keep him around as a friend.

DATING WHEN YOU'RE TRANS

Transgender teens have a slightly different situation. For one, not all people will get what it means to be trans, and some may feel confused about what it means to date someone who doesn't identify with their biological gender. Trans dating can also get complicated if you are already passing for a different gender and the object of your affection doesn't know you are trans. Your date could feel betrayed after finding out, thinking that you presented yourself on the outside as something different than what your physical body looks like naked (at least for now). It's really important to make sure that the person you are dating knows you are trans and is open to dating someone trans—or you'll both get hurt.

That being said, more people are open to dating trans people than you think! Sometimes it just takes a little while for your crush to get used to the idea.

So how to bring up the topic? Every situation is unique, and there are no hard and fast rules to follow. You could bring it up right off, which would be fairly easy if you meet in a queer setting, like a GSA meeting or at a local queer youth event, since everyone is talking about their personal experiences. You could also wait a few dates and just get to know each other casually first (or hang out with a group of friends). But if you've gone out a couple of times and your date still doesn't know that you're trans, you should talk about it before things get physical.

You may want to practice this reveal with supportive friends first so you feel more comfortable about any potential reactions. Try starting the conversation with phrases like, "I feel really great when we're together, and I want to share something about me with you" or "I want to tell you something that I think you're cool enough to handle." These approaches may make things go smoother than just blurting it out or trying to slip hints. The important thing to remember is that you're not revealing some terrible secret. Rather, you're sharing a wonderful part of yourself with someone you're interested in. It's a sign of personal integrity that you can be open about your life.

If you "prescreened" your date by seeing if he or she is open to trans dating before you went out, things will probably go well. Even if you haven't, you may receive a positive reaction—you certainly deserve one! People might also say they think being trans is cool but that they aren't into it or they may ask you to give them some time to process it and understand better what that means. Unfortunately, there have also been cases where someone hearing the news has gotten upset, even violent. It's less likely that this will occur if your date is queer-friendly or if the relationship hasn't gotten very far yet. But just in case, you may want to have the conversation in a public place.

FRIENDS OR MORE THAN FRIENDS?
Another thing that comes along with queer dating is the fine line between friendship and romantic interest.

Dating on the Down Low

As you know by now, queer dating isn't always like a scene out of a Hollywood romantic comedy, where couples are freely strolling through parks or one teen is getting picked up at the front door by a date for the prom. A lot of queer dating happens when no one is looking. One of you may not be out to your parents or at school, or you both may not be ready to hold hands in public. You should never out someone before they are ready. The situation can be frustrating and take time to resolve, but sometimes you might need to date in secret. This may mean sharing lunch at a restaurant away from your neighborhood, introducing your date to people as your friend, or calling your romantic interest after your parents have gone to bed. We're not suggesting that deceit is a good way to live; it's not. But your security has to come first. If the world around you makes it impossible to date or hang out with other queer teens, you'll have to find your own way to do it.

In high school, a lot of our friends are just naturally the same gender. For queer teens, that creates extra opportunities for a friend-crush to develop unexpectedly. You may think you're just hanging out with someone as pals and suddenly feel sparks. Or you may discover that a longtime friend who you never even considered dating has harbored a deep crush on you this whole time — and you didn't know!

It's true that sometimes friends make the best relationship material. But sometimes a friend is … just a friend.

So take it slow, keep assessing the situation and your feelings, and never feel pressured to do anything you're not comfortable with. If you start to feel something deeper than friendship with someone and wonder if they feel the same, you can let them know in a casual way, like, "We know each other so well, maybe we should just date already! Ha, ha!" See what the reaction is. Sure, you may be worried that bringing up the topic could ruin your friendship, and we're not gonna lie to you: It can be awkward for a while if your crush doesn't reciprocate. But true friendships will survive. If things get a little weird, give the person some space and come back to the friendship with the clear intention to keep it platonic.

UM, SO, UH, WANNA HANG OUT SOMETIME?

You figured out that your crush is queer-friendly, and you're pretty sure you like her/him—a lot. Awesome. Now what? It's time to make your move. Here's a handy four-step guide to asking someone out. (We use a girl as an example, but it works for anyone!)

- ✪ Approach your crush when she's by herself. Ask how she's doing. Flirt a little. Make a joke or some comment to put her at ease, like "Hey, great jacket! Where do you get that?" or "Did you see the look on Mr. Kennedy's face when I said that Venezuela was the second planet in the solar system?"

- ✪ Mention an activity that you'd like to ask her to do. "Have you seen the new Drew Barrymore movie?"

"I hear there are some hot bands playing in the park this weekend." "My cousin is hosting an open mic night next weekend at my church."

✲ Ask her to join you. "I was thinking of going, would you like to go with me?"

✲ Wait for her response. If she says, yes, great! Tell her you'll call or text with the details. If she says no, don't ask why, just say "OK, cool". If she's interested, she'll probably suggest another time to hang out. If she just lets it go, her heart may be somewhere else.

My First Real Date

I lived in a place where not a lot of other teens were out, so naturally, the minute any other male expressed even one iota of curiosity, my girlfriends had us married already. They kept telling me I had to meet this guy Rory. I'd hung out with other gay guys before, but only casually, and I had no idea how to date other than what I saw on TV. My friend Tanisha arranged for us to have a blind date at a kind of fancy restaurant and then succeeded in making me freak out about everything, from what I was going to wear to what we were going to eat.

I ended up going to meet Rory with a big bunch of expensive flowers, a heart-shaped box of chocolates, and a mix of gooey love songs that I hated. In formal wear. It was way too much too soon. Luckily, Rory realized I was really nervous and had never been on a date before, so we ended up just laughing about it. We eventually became good friends, but after that I realized that I didn't have to bring a bunch of clichés with me on a date (or let my friends control my love life). My relaxed and stylish self, plus a few casual flourishes—like telling him he's a good listener, or opening the door for him—were all that was needed to make a pleasant evening.

THE WOE OF REJECTION

Getting rejected sucks. Especially if you really took a risk and put yourself out there. Sometimes the best thing to do is to walk away and give yourself space. Vent to a trusted friend about what happened, cry if you need to. And then, when you're done wallowing, get out of the house. Go to a movie or for a run. Hang out with some friends whom you can count on to make you laugh. Although it might be hard not to take it personally, most likely this isn't about you but where the other person is at. Eventually you will find someone else whom you'll want to ask out. Romantic rejection is part of life, like not making the cut for the team or the school play. It feels really crappy, but it also reminds you that you are alive. If you let the fear of rejection rule you, you'll basically never do anything. Ever. Now what kind of life would that be?

GREAT FIRST DATE IDEAS

If you've secured a date, you'll need a place to go. A great first date is all about sharing in a fun yet relaxing activity—no parasailing or scuba diving yet!—that will give you the opportunity to get to know someone better, see if there is a vibe between you, and find out if you want to have a second date. Awkwardness and nervousness are to be expected, especially if you're really into the other person. What to do on a first date? Here are a few ideas.

- ⊗ Movies. While this can seem like a cliché, movies are a popular date activity for a reason. They give you something to focus on other than each other and something to talk about when they're over.

- ⊗ An activity you both enjoy. Try skateboarding, video games, Dance Dance Revolution at the arcade, a bike ride, or a play.

- ⊗ A gay-friendly spot for coffee or an underage club for live bands.

- ⊗ Something chill, like hanging out in the park to watch the sunset or walking around downtown or at the mall.

There are also places you might want to avoid on a first date, such as a school dance or function or anywhere you know a lot of your friends will be. You want to make sure you get face time with your date without all your girls/boys around, making fools of themselves.

IF SOMEONE ASKS *YOU* OUT

It's always flattering to find out that someone's interested in you. Often it's a complete surprise and you're totally caught off guard. Here you are, working together on a PowerPoint presentation for your US government class, and suddenly Shawn the Jock is asking you to the beach next weekend. Whoa. It can be tempting to freak out, but stay cool and assess the situation. Don't play games. If you're interested, just say yes. Making someone chase you just because you want attention is lame, and he might lose interest. If you're not sure whether you like him, give him a shot. Remember, it took a lot of guts for him to approach you. Hanging out for an hour or two may reveal a side of him you never knew existed. If you agree to something simple and not too time-consuming, you don't have much to lose.

Top Retro LGBT Teen Date Movies

The late 1990s saw a good number of films for LGBT teens. Rent these for some great queer dating inspiration!

- The Incredibly True Adventures of Two Girls in Love (1995)
- But I'm a Cheerleader (1999)
- Beautiful Thing (1996)
- All Over Me (1997)
- Edge of Seventeen (1998)
- Show Me Love (1998)

Of course, if the person is totally not attractive to you or, worse, creeps you out, you really should say no. It's not nice to lead someone on whom you have no interest in, or who is creepy or weird. The best thing to do is to tell him that you appreciate the offer but would rather just be friends. Sure, it's hard to say that to someone—you know it would suck to hear it yourself—but what are the alternatives? Saying you're busy or have other plans? Telling a little white lie may seem like an easy way out, but it also leaves him an opening to ask you out again— not to mention the possibility that he might catch you in a fib. And if you overreact and act mean just to make sure the message gets across, then you deprive yourself of a queer ally and potential source of support.

MAKING IT PAST DATE ONE

So you finally scored a date with that hottie you've been crushing on for months. Whew! Give yourself a 10 out of 10 for guts, poise, and grace. Getting to this point was hard enough; you don't want to screw it up now. Here are some pointers that will help you score a second date (if you decide that your date is worthy of your fine self, of course).

◉ **Keep it short.** This is a first date, not the Ironman triathlon. Go for coffee, ice cream, or a burrito. This way, if things don't go well, you're not stuck all day or night with a boring date. And if things do go well, you'll leave your date wanting more.

⊚ **Don't advertise.** Don't blab all over your digital space or tell everyone within earshot about your upcoming date. And do not change your profile status or send out constant updates about your progress, even if you're happier than a Trekkie at a sci-fi convention. Word could get back to him pretty easily and put a lot of pressure on the date. Plus, it's, um, kind of immature.

Is It a Date?

Sometime you have a plan to hang out with someone, but you don't know if it's actually a date. He may just want to hang out and scope other dudes. Or maybe she just didn't want to go to the dance/club/mall alone. How can you know?

It's probably a date if the other person:

⊚ seems nervous

⊚ has not invited anyone else along

⊚ dresses a little nicer than usual

⊚ makes some sort of physical contact, like reaching for your hand

⊚ asks you to slow dance

⊚ offers to pay for whatever you're doing (i.e., dinner, the movie tickets, etc.)

⊚ tries to kiss you at the end of the night

If it's not immediately obvious whether this is actually a date, don't stress too much. Instead, try to just have fun. You'll both figure it out eventually.

⊚ **Power off.** You might think she'll be impressed with the number of times your cell phone goes off in one night or how many texts you're getting. Boy, aren't you popular?! The question is, does she care? She'll be more impressed if you focus your attention on *her*. This is your chance for some real face time. Turn off your cell phone and put it out of sight.

⊚ **Break the ice.** A first date can be clunky, and you may need to get the conversational ball rolling. Have a few starter topics. What kind of music have you been listening to lately? What's your favorite blog? Where did you go last weekend? These are the kinds of things that can lead to deeper conversations.

⊚ **Keep it light.** Don't rush into the TMI (too much information) zone or get too serious. The purpose of a first date is to get to know your date and to have fun, not bring on the drama. Of course, you can talk about what's going on in your life, but do you really need to go on and on about how you're failing every class or how you keep getting nasty zits on your legs? You can get more personal later—if and when the relationship gets more serious.

I once had an ingrown hair this long growing out of my...

⊚ **Privacy rules.** Don't take her to a place where all your friends hang out. You asked her on a date because you want to get to know her. You don't need your goofy BFF making faces at you from across the room (jealous!) or interrupting your conversation. And she doesn't want to feel ambushed and out of her element. Go someplace you both feel comfortable, where you can talk in private.

⊚ **Leave your ex out.** It's OK to mention whether you've been out for a while and had previous relationships, but if you keep talking about what an evil ass your former boyfriend was or how your ex-girlfriend broke your heart when you split up, it might scare your date away. Plus, didn't you ask her out because you're over your pathetic ex?

⊚ **Take it slow.** It's a first date, nothing more. Be optimistic, but don't set yourself up for a fall. He may bring you the moon and stars eventually, but making plans to go to the same college or picking out your future cats' names right off the bat is a sure sign that things are moving too fast—and that may mean trouble down the line.

⊚ **Don't play games.** You should be dating this person because you are truly attracted to and interested in her, even if you only end up as friends. Using someone to show off or to make another person jealous is super lame and will probably come back to bite you in the butt.

- ⑥ **Stay classy.** Show up on time and be courteous to your date and to any wait staff you encounter. Show your best side, even if things aren't going well and you're pretty sure there won't be a second date. You never know: Even if things don't work out romantically, he may have a friend who interests you!

- ⑥ **Try not to judge.** The person across from you is probably just as nervous as you are. She's putting herself on the line, too! Just because she's wearing too much perfume or she's talking a little too much about how cute her baby sister is doesn't mean all bets are off. As she gets more comfortable with you and you both find a groove, you may find that the little things take a back seat to the bigger picture.

- ⑥ **Forget about typical roles.** Queer dating can be confusing, but a lot of people make it harder than it should be by trying to invent expectations based on tired gender stereotypes. If she's girly, are you supposed to be butch? Who opens the door for whom? Who pays? Don't worry about all that. Without strict gender roles, same-sex relationships can feel more equal. There are fewer expectations about who should pay for the date, who should make the first move,

or who should hold the door. The great thing about queer dating is that you get to make it up as you go along. Just be yourself and go with your feelings. Hopefully your date will do the same, and you'll be able to figure it all out together.

◎ **End on a high note.** If everything went well—and even if it didn't—remember to thank your date for the evening. If you really like her, you can send a cute, short text later as well to say that you had a good time.

ON THE QUEER FRONTIER   2008

GOING FOR GOLD

You may have noticed that there aren't a whole lot of queer athlete role models, but that's not because there aren't a lot of queer athletes. Many of them—including tennis star Billie Jean King, Olympic diver Greg Louganis, baseball player Billy Beane, and football players David Kopay and Esera Tuaolo—have simply waited to come out until after their careers were over. But that's starting to change. Tennis legend Martina Navratilova came out in 1981, and basketball player Sheryl Swoopes came out in 2005, both during their professional careers. More recently, proudly out Australian diver Matthew Mitcham made headlines around the world when he won the gold medal for 10-meter platform diving in the 2008 Olympics in Beijing. Matthew has since inspired many young queer athletes to come out and to follow their professional dreams.

My Disastrous First Date With Kate

I was a freshman in college and hadn't dated too many people when I met Kate. She was a friend of a friend and started coming around a lot whenever we would hang out. I thought she was kind of cute, and I could tell she was interested in me.

She asked me to go to a community choir concert with her. I was excited because she seemed nice and I knew a lot of cool people would be there. The snow started falling as we headed out the door. By the time the concert let out, a foot or more was on the ground. A friend dropped us off at my apartment. I was feeling happy from the concert and the pretty coating of snow. Perhaps that's why I invited her in. We kissed a little before I told her she'd better get going if she was going to catch the last bus home. She reluctantly put on her coat and headed out into the night.

A half-hour later, she knocked on my door, saying she had missed her bus and it was snowing too hard to call for a ride. Could she spend the night? I was almost asleep by then, but I let her in. She tried to crawl into my bed with me, but I set her up with blankets and a pillow on the couch. She was still sleeping the next morning when I left for school and swimming practice. When I got home, I was horrified to find Kate in my room, sitting up in my bed! She said she had a migraine and was too sick to go home. And then she tried to kiss me! I pushed her away, found $10 in my dresser, called a cab, and sent her home. I couldn't believe that she actually called me the next day to ask me out again. After that, I was a lot more careful about who I invited back to my apartment!

GOING FOR DATE TWO

Your first date went swimmingly—he even laughed when you told him he had spinach in his teeth—and you'd really like to go out with him again. Well, go ahead and ask. Wait until the end of your first date, of course, and then say something romantic but straightforward, like, "I had fun tonight, and I'm really enjoying getting to know you. Want to do it again?" If he says yes, great. Ask for his phone number if you don't already have it and call to set up something later in the week. Don't wait too long, though. Some people think it's best to wait at least three days before you call someone, but if you really like him, don't keep him hanging.

If he says no when you ask or says yes but then offers an excuse when you call, take it at face value and chalk it up to experience. If he hesitates or says he'd rather call you, that's OK. Sometimes it takes a while for people to process how they feel about things, even if they've had an amazing time. Try not to get overly anxious waiting for the call by keeping busy with your own life and not checking your phone every two minutes. If he doesn't call after a week, he probably won't. Just let it go. Some people aren't good at being direct, which is unfortunate, but you can cut your losses by moving on and not obsessing over why he never contacted you again.

WHAT TO DO IF THE DATE SUCKS

You were sure you and Joni would hit it off. She's so cute, working behind the scenes of the school play, dressed all in black. You always share a laugh about the drama behind the drama club. So it was a total surprise when she sat across from you on your first date, texting with her cousin about some lame reality show. WTF?

Or maybe you said or did something you think was incredibly embarrassing, like spilling a latte on your pants, telling a joke that completely bombed, or getting into a little argument about politics. Before asking for the check or assuming that your love life will always be sitcom material, take a moment to consider that the date might not be going as badly as it seems. First dates are awkward and not always the best indicator of whether or not you've found your soulmate. If you think there might be some potential there, stick with it; some people need two or three dates to find out if someone's right for them.

That said, things won't always work out. Even if the date isn't a complete disaster, one or both of you may notice early on that there's no chemistry. If the conversation comes to a complete halt or your date is doing something gross with her food or the minutes are dragging by slower than an algebra class in springtime, you may want to cut the date short.

But how? Sometimes the other person feels the same way, and you can just finish up your smoothie and say, "Thanks for hanging out. See you around!" and it'll be cool. But if you sense your date is more into you than you are into her, it can be tricky to disengage. Be honest! Don't say something lame, like you forgot you had other plans or you're feeling sick. Politely thank her for the evening and say you need to go. If she asks why, it's OK to say that you appreciated your time together, but for some reason you're just not feeling it. Don't promise to call if that's not what you intend. Being up front about your feelings early on is better than being trapped in a web of guilt and lies later and shows that you're a confident person who cares about others' feelings. You'll be so proud of the way you handled things that you may just want to date yourself.

SIX

GETTING TOGETHER

QUEER
RELATIONSHIPS

You've met someone! You've hung out for a while, had four or five dates, and are really into each other. This person seems perfect for you. Just as great, she's totally smitten with you as well. You go together like two queer peas in a perfectly decorated pod. Is it time to take the next step? What is the next step? Going steady? Going out? Picking out matching wedding dresses? Getting matching rainbow tats?

The best question to ask yourself is what are *you* looking for? That's a biggie, and it can sometimes take a long time and some emotional experience to discover the answer. There's a reason all those pop divas sell millions of records singing about the search for love. Everyone can relate. It takes time, energy, and yes, probably some heartbreak, too, before you find someone you really connect with. And even then, you'll probably try out all sorts of relationships before you find the one that's right for you and the person you're with. Remember: She may not know exactly what she's looking for either.

The most important thing to keep in mind is don't rush. There's no need to hurry up and plan out your retirement together in Palm Springs. Take your time. Enjoy just being together right now. If starting a relationship feels like too much pressure, then wait until the time is right. You'll know it when you feel it.

If you do feel you're ready to take it to another level with your sweetie, how do you do it? Sometimes two people just fall into a relationship naturally, as a consequence of having so much fun together. Sometimes it's more formal: One person asks another to make it official that they're going out. Either way, you should make sure that you both say it out loud at some point to avoid any confusion or hurt feelings down the line. We've known plenty of people who thought they were going out with someone, only to find out at some point that the other person had no idea!

Relationships come in many flavors and, like snowflakes or pancakes, no two are exactly alike. Yet they all require focus and dedication. Sometimes they can seem scary, but you'll find that with some patience, the right person, and the right amount of communication, you can easily form the kind of bond that's right for both of you. Your relationship will always be what you and your partner make it, and that will be a unique blend of happiness and craziness every time you are with someone new.

WHAT IS A QUEER RELATIONSHIP?

Deciding whether or not to start a queer relationship — or even knowing what a queer relationship is — can be confusing. Queer relationships exist in just as many different varieties as straight ones, but there may not be any obvious examples of queer relationships around for you to follow. Because queer people were traditionally (and sometimes still are) forced to stay in the closet, they have never been front and center in the media or on the street. That's one of the reasons why the fight for same-sex marriage rights is so important to a lot of people. It helps the public to recognize the huge amount of healthy, long-term queer relationships all around us.

One good thing about not having been inundated with representations of queer couples in magazines and on TV is that there are no rules to follow (short of being loving and respectful to each other, of course). You're free to define the kind of relationship that works for you and your partner and to invent something completely unique. You're also free to have the same traditional relationship your parents or your friends' parents might have. The important thing is to do what makes your heart happy.

WHY HAVE A RELATIONSHIP?

You don't have to plan your future around having a relationship — or even have one at all. Plenty of people enjoy being single, and it's OK to concentrate on getting your own life together, waiting until the time is right for you to enter into a commitment with another person.

All that said, relationships are awesome experiences and can be a lot of fun. It's natural to want to take it to another level with someone you care about. One of the main purposes of starting an official relationship is to find out if those feelings are lasting and real. Can they survive getting closer to someone, or is it better for both of you to go back to being good friends who shared something meaningful for a while? Do you make a good team for facing life's ups and downs? Can you be there for each other in a deeper sense? In many cases, you'll never know until you try.

Being Single

There's a lot of pressure out there to have a relationship. But going out with someone when you're young isn't for everyone—especially if you're still trying to figure out who you are as a person. Some people don't feel the need to pursue relationships until they're older (some never do at all), and that's OK. Even if it seems like everyone around you is going out with someone, it's perfectly fine to wait until you're ready or until you find some-one you're attracted to in that way. Staying single can be fulfilling in its own way, giving you time to focus on other things, like sports, your studies, or your family. And if you don't want to be single but it seems like it's taking forever to meet someone, have patience—it will happen.

ARE YOU READY?

Is it time for you to enter relationship territory? Before you decide that having a relationship with someone is right for you, ask yourself these questions.

◎ Do I want to be in a relationship just because I'm lonely?

◎ Do I want to be in a relationship only because everyone else is?

◎ Am I saying yes just because someone is asking and I don't want to hurt her?

Obviously, if your answer is yes to any of these questions, then you need to reconsider. You would be treating the other person unfairly if you were in it just for the relationship and not for him or her. You want to go out with a *person*, not an idea. And going out with someone because you feel pressured to do so is never a good thing.

You don't need a relationship to make you feel good about yourself. You need to take responsibility for your own happiness. Sometimes when you're queer, it can feel like you're all alone in the world. So when you meet someone and hit it off, you may feel that quickly latching on to that person will solve all your problems. Reality check, darling: That's not going to happen. Believe in yourself first, and everything else will follow.

Also, remember that even though they say love conquers all, they also say love is blind. Take a moment to step back from the heart-racing fires of your new dreamy romance and consider your potential mate objectively—as relationship material. Is he ready for a relationship? Does she seem stable enough to bring positive things to the relationship? Can you trust him to be open and responsible enough to handle it? You deserve to be with someone who respects you for the wonderful creature you are and brings out the best in you.

If you believe that you're both in a great place to start a relationship adventure together, then go for it! The next step is finding out what kind of relationship works for you.

Dating Someone Much Older

Let's face it: Depending on where you live, there may not be many other LGBT teens around. So when that cute twenty-five-year-old from the coffee shop asks you out, you might want to say yes. Or you might be infatuated with someone older: your coach, a church counselor, or a friend of your parents. That's really common, and it may feel flattering that an older person is giving you attention. But this kind of relationship comes with a lot of risks. Sometimes, older people want to date younger people because they believe that they can more easily control the relationship. And then there's the issue of legality. Adults are not legally allowed to have sex with minors (see more about this in Chapter 7), and you could both get in big trouble with the law.

Unfortunately, many young queers who are looking for an older role model do end up in these kinds of relationships. It's fine—and even good—to have older role models, but it's best to date people your own age.

MAPPING IT OUT

So what kind of relationship do you want? Many relationships evolve naturally, and you may not even know what kind of relationship you want until you're actually in one! But when you do enter into a relationship, you can avoid a lot of grief about "unwritten rules" by thinking about your expectations and making sure they gel with your partner's. This means actually talking about it. Of course, people don't always like to have conversations about their relationships. After all, you're totally hot for each other; you should just know what one another is thinking telepathically, right? Right, and you're the king of Norway. Being honest from the start can keep things from getting confusing later.

Relationship Rules

1. Romantic dinner once a week.

2. eyes ONLY on each other.

3. no pink muscle tees.

Does your idea of a relationship include eating lunch together each day and talking on the phone every night? Or does it mean an occasional text message and heavy make-out sessions on Fridays? If you're trans, would your partner prefer that you always dress as one gender? If you're gay, does your boyfriend expect you to drop all your other male friends? (This would be a big red flag, by the way.) Will you tell your parents about each other? If this is your first relationship, you might not even know exactly what you want. The important thing is to pay attention to your feelings and to talk about them with your partner.

You'll also need to talk, at some point, about commitment. You may decide to start just "seeing" each other or "hanging out"—which usually means dating without any commitment. (Although be careful about any assumptions!) But as things get serious, you may want to define your relationship more precisely.

That could mean not dating or hooking up with other people, which would make it an exclusive relationship. (If you are having sex with each other and decide to not have sex with anyone else, you can also call it *monogamous*.)

If you decide you are not ready or willing to be exclusive, that's fine, too. Just make sure you and your partner are on the same page and agree to the rules. Are you allowed to make out with other people? Go out on dates with other people? Sleep with other people? Be really specific so that no one feels betrayed. As your relationship grows, things may change, depending on how you both feel. No rules are right or wrong, but you and your partner have to agree on them. It's not called cheating because you dated or slept with someone else but because it went against a relationship rule. Establish the rules together and stick to them if you want to have a healthy, respectful relationship. Read more about the sexual implications of being exclusive or not in Chapter 7.

My Big, Bad Lesbian Breakup

Alice was the perfect girl for me. We were friends, and I'd had a crush on her for a long time before we finally got together. We had so much in common, plus she was smart and cute and sexy. We were going to different colleges when we started dating, so we visited each other a couple of times and made plans to live together over the summer. When the semester was over, I packed up my things and got a crappy job and a dingy sublet not far from where she lived in her college town. But I didn't care; we were together, and things were great. Until two weeks after I arrived when she dumped me.

I couldn't believe it. I'd given up my whole summer to move there, and now I was alone and depressed and couldn't ever imagine being happy again. I sleepwalked through my door-to-door canvassing job, barely caring if people talked to me or not. I didn't want to do any of the things I normally enjoyed. What fun would dancing be if she weren't there? I didn't seem to have the strength to pull my bike out of the garage. Food tasted bland, and I subsisted on boxed macaroni and cheese and corn flakes. I pulled the drapes and turned the lights off in my apartment and played the same Melissa Etheridge CD again and again. I cried myself to sleep each night. I was miserable and didn't think I would ever meet someone I would love as much as Alice.

Well, that miserable summer finally ended, and I made my way back to school. I got involved in a new organization on campus, and soon I had a new group of friends and was barely thinking about Alice anymore. It took about a year, but finally, I did start dating someone whom I really cared about. Now, I hardly ever think about the girl I thought I couldn't live without.

LEARNING TO COMMUNICATE

Good communication is key in a relationship, but when you're young, it can be tough. For instance, you may feel vulnerable and not be into telling your girlfriend that you were jealous when she went out with her basketball team last Friday instead of you. But it's best to be open about your feelings (in a gentle, nonaccusatory way, that is). If you don't say anything, she may never know you were upset. The same goes if she does or says something that makes you feel sad or uncomfortable. Don't bottle it up inside or act like a martyr. Be brave and discuss things rationally in a private space where you both feel comfortable. Maybe practice what you're going to say beforehand until you can say it calmly. And if you've done something that you know is out of bounds, own up to it. You'll find that talking things out really makes a difference, and you'll respect each other even more than you already do. And communication doesn't always have to be about the bad stuff! Remember to talk about the good things in your relationship as well, and don't forget to compliment your partner when she's done something great or offer encouragement when she's going through difficult times.

Learning to communicate with each other takes practice. You don't need to process every little thing or stay up all night trying to figure out if your relationship is healthy. But checking in regularly about how things are going certainly helps. Even if you're not always on the same page, you can at least make sure you're reading the same book.

IS IT LOVE?

He's so cute, he has amazing style, he really listens to what you have to say, and you can't ever imagine getting tired of that adorable way he scrunches up his nose when he does math in his head. He sings you old country songs over the phone before you go to sleep, and you both like weird cult Japanese movies—especially the ones with really fake-looking monsters. You've even decided that you're officially going out.

But all of that doesn't necessarily mean you're in love. Sometimes we just get infatuated with people but there's no real substance or maturity behind the emotions. To see if you are really in love, ask yourself these questions.

Does it seem mutual?

Can you trust your partner with your secrets?

Do you bring out the best in each other?

Are you confident about the relationship?

Are you happy?

Does the relationship make your life better?

Would you willingly give your partner your last donut hole, even though you'd been saving it for later?

You're my Kentucky cowboy / You get my heart a' galloping....

If you can honestly answer yes to these questions, chances are this is more than just an infatuation. Of course, sometimes it's hard to tell if it's real love when you're in the middle of it. But if you mostly feel like a better person when you're in his or her presence, then we say it's probably love ... or something like it.

ON THE QUEER FRONTIER

2004

WEDDING BELLS ARE RINGING

Queer marriage has never been recognized by the federal government. We've had commitment ceremonies and, in recent years, have also gained certain domestic partnership rights, but a marriage license has remained a dream. In recent years, however, things have (slowly!) started to change. On February 12, 2004, San Francisco began issuing marriage licenses to same-sex couples. Thousands of couples lined up at San Francisco City Hall over Valentine's Day weekend (Kathy and her partner were among them!) to get married. Soon cities around the country followed suit, including Portland, Oregon; New Paltz, New York; and Ashbury Park, New Jersey. However, in subsequent court rulings, all of those marriages were deemed invalid. Today, same sex marriage is legal in several states, including Massachusetts, Vermont, and Iowa. There's still a long fight ahead, but at least it's now an issue at the forefront of American politics.

MEETING THE PARENTS

Besides taking the SATs, there's not much that is more stressful than meeting your girlfriend or boyfriend's parents for the first time. Here are some tips to ensure that things go smoothly.

- ◎ **Know what you're walking into.** Is she out to her parents? Does she have two gay dads? Do her parents head up the local PFLAG chapter? Or do they attend the Love Won Out antigay conference every year? Are you just a friend? Or do her parents know all the salacious details of your relationship? (Well, hopefully not *all* of the salacious details.) The more you know, the better you can prepare yourself for the event.

- ◎ **Pull out the tie and jacket.** Well, that might be going a bit overboard, but do dress a little nicer and more conservatively than you would normally. Save the "Zombie Death Squad" T-shirt for the school dance and put on your nicest jeans and sweater.

- ◎ **Make eye contact and speak in full sentences.** Look her parents in the eye and say hello. If they ask you about yourself, even if you're shy, try to give answers that consist of more than one word. If you're trans and her parents address you with the wrong pronoun, smile and politely correct them. ("I prefer 'he,' thank you!") You don't need to pretend that you're on the speech team, but do let them see some of your glowing personality.

◉ **Help out!** If you're invited for dinner, be sure to offer to help set the table, do the dishes, or clear the table. Even if your boyfriend sits on his big fat tush, you can impress them by showing that you have manners.

◉ **Join in.** If the family gathers around the TV to watch football or invites you play a rousing game of Scrabble, do your best to join in. Even if you don't know a corner back from the corner store or if spelling is your worst subject, you'll still win points for being a good sport.

⊚ **Keep it down with the PDA.** Even if your girlfriend is out and proud and her parents march in the gay pride parade every year, keep your hands to yourself on this first visit. Discuss with your girlfriend beforehand what she's comfortable with in terms of hugging, handholding, and kissing in front of her folks.

⊚ **Understand the rules.** Is he allowed to have boyfriends in his room? Does his family say prayers before eating? Get as much information beforehand as you can so you can abide by house rules.

Keep the Romance Alive

The fact that you're in a relationship doesn't mean you can slack off on the romance. No one's waited a lifetime for a boring relationship! Of course, going out to dinner and long walks in the park together may get stale after awhile. And how many dozens of roses does one person need? If you feel like you're falling into a rut, embark on a fun project together. Build a fan site, learn to cook Moroccan food, start a fantasy football team. Don't be afraid to do something different that takes you out of your comfort zone. If she's really into rock climbing, but you're scared of heights, be brave and take a class at the rock climbing gym. Go to an all night rave or try camping, if that's what he loves to do. Be spontaneous. Surprise each other. Get creative. Treat your relationship like a blog or scrapbook that you want to fill up with awesome memories, quirky thoughts, and meaningful experiences.

◉ **Keep it short.** Don't overstay your welcome. You came for dinner or to introduce yourself—but not to spend the night! Make a good first impression, but go home at a reasonable hour. That's the best way to ensure you'll be asked to come over again!

US AGAINST THE WORLD

Being a queer couple definitely has its perks: sharing clothes, making out in the bathroom, endless snuggles. But it can also be a challenge. In some parts of the country, teens are still fighting to be able to take same-sex dates to the prom or even to hold hands on school grounds. In some private schools you can be expelled for having a queer relationship. It's pretty ridiculous. Then there are occasional awkward social moments. Should you grind on him on the dance floor like everyone else is doing with their partners? Should you kiss her hello when she comes off the softball field after a game? You have to think twice before doing things everyone else does freely, which is annoying and unfair.

On top of that, it can seem like no one understands your love. Your mom may think it's just a phase. Your friends like your girlfriend well enough but don't know how she fits into your clique. And her sister, well, she'll do anything to keep you two apart. What do you do when faced with such obstacles?

It's very common in queer teen relationships to get super insular. No one cares for you like she does. No one understands you like her. So you end up dropping all your friends and spend time with her 24/7. But that's neither good nor healthy. For one, it reinforces to everyone that you've "changed" since you started being with her, which is not the message you want to send. And two, you've got to have separate interests to keep yourselves interesting to each other.

Avoid falling into what is known as the Urge to Merge. If you spend too much time together, you'll set up unrealistic expectations, rely too much on one another, and end up smothering each other. One day you'll look in the mirror and realize that you dress alike, have the same hair, and worst of all, only talk in "we" statements. Ick. You were looking for a romantic partner, not an identical twin. And what happens if you ever fight or break up? If you've dumped all your friends, you may have no one to turn to for support. And then you'll *really* feel alone.

LEARN TO FIGHT FAIR

It's true: Into every sunny queer relationship a little rain must fall. Squabbles, sulks, spats, and full-on fights are normal, even if neither of you can remember what the problem was to begin with. And is it really worth ruining your relationship over basically nothing? Here are some tips for venting your frustration without doing damage you'll regret later.

◉ **Never fight when others are present.** Save the public drama for the school play. Ask your boyfriend if you can talk about what's bugging you somewhere private. Making a scene is never productive.

◉ **Take a time out.** If things are getting too hot, get out of there. Don't just walk out and slam the door, though. Stop, take a deep breath, offer to talk about things once you've both calmed down, and leave for a few minutes to take a walk around the block or to gather your thoughts in the other room.

◉ **Choose your words.** Yes, it's hard to control yourself when you're angry, but it's out of bounds to hit below the belt with your words by bringing up deep and intimate secrets, using racial or sexual slurs, or going overboard and blaming everything in the world on your partner. Say the wrong thing just once, and you can ruin an entire relationship. Cruel words stay imprinted in people's minds for what sometimes seems like eternity.

◉ **Never get physical.** Hitting someone is physical abuse and doing so will ruin everything. You'll not only harm your partner and betray any trust in the relationship, but you can also wind up in trouble with the law. Even raising your hand as a threat shows that you might think about resorting to violence, so don't do it. If you feel the urge to get physical, go outside and punch a rock, scream into a pillow, or do whatever it takes to get out your anger in a nonharmful way.

IS YOUR RELATIONSHIP HEALTHY?

Not sure if your relationship is healthy? Take this quiz. (Substitute the pronouns with the one your partner goes by.)

1 When you think of him:
   a. You get a warm feeling all over.
   b. You get a special stirring in your loins.
   c. Um, he's all I ever think about.

2 When you hang out with your friends:
   a. She's with her own friends.
   b. She's my only friend.
   c. She gets jealous.

3 When you do something stupid:
   a. He laughs along with you.
   b. He announces it to all of your friends.
   c. He berates you and calls you names.

4 When she's being romantic she:
   a. Makes a mixed CD of love songs.
   b. Calls you her little marshmallow head.
   c. Tells you if you leave, she'll kill herself.

5 When you don't go with him to something he invited you to he:

  a. Tries not to rub it in, but tells you what a great time you missed.

  b. Says you owe him one and reminds you of it constantly.

  c. Throws a temper tantrum and storms out of your house.

6 She sees you laughing with a girl in your homeroom. She:

  a. Smiles, waves hello, and waits for you to finish so you can go to lunch together.

  b. Tries to join in the conversation to see what's so funny.

  c. Demands to know who she is and accuses you of cheating.

7 He says he's going to the movies with his boys. You:

  a. Tell him to call you tomorrow to tell you how it was.

  b. Pout because you wanted to see that movie with him.

  c. Sneak into the back of the movie theater to make sure he's really there and that no cute guys are with him.

8 You just got some bad news. She hears about it and says:

   a. "Baby, I'll be right over," and shows up with tissues and ice cream.

   b. "Oh, does that mean we aren't going bowling tonight?"

   c. "You think that's bad; wait until you hear about my day."

9 You show up in a new outfit. He says:

   a. "You look so sexy!"

   b. "I don't care about your shirt so long as it's off you."

   c. "That shirt looks stupid."

10 You just joined the lacrosse team. She:

   a. Asks for your schedule so she can come to cheer you on.

   b. Hangs around outside of practice, waiting for you.

   c. Tells you to quit immediately because you won't have any time to spend with her.

If you answered mostly As, congratulations! You've got a healthy start of a relationship to build on. You two seem to support each other in positive ways, and you both have your own lives. The key to a fulfilling relationship is to balance your time together with time pursuing your own interests, and you seem to be doing that well. And you haven't let your other friends drop off. That's important, too.

If you answered mostly Bs, you both may be a little immature for a relationship. Each of you seems to think of yourself before the other, and you're kind of clingy and infatuated. Perhaps you like the *idea* of being in a relationship better than actually being in one. Remember, relationships are about give and take, compromise, and being there for the other person—not just getting your own needs met. Work on trying to put your partner's feelings before your own at least 50 percent of the time. If you find you can't do that, maybe you're just not ready for a relationship yet. That's OK—this might be a time for you to focus on yourself. Just be honest about that.

If you answered mostly Cs, we're worried about you. This relationship has some serious red flags and is possibly abusive. There are signs of controlling behavior, obsession, and manipulation. If your partner doesn't love you for who you are, trust you, or respect your time with your friends—or vice versa—you'll never get anywhere. It's best to get out of this relationship and then examine why you were in it in the first place. With a little bit of growth and self-reflection, you're bound to find a healthier relationship next time.

IF A RELATIONSHIP EVER GETS ABUSIVE

Unfortunately, not all queer relationships are good news, and some relationship problems are actually pretty serious. If you feel like you are in an abusive relationship, you probably are. If you're not sure, ask yourself these questions.

- Does he yell at you often for things you didn't do?
- Does she abuse alcohol or drugs?
- Does he hit you?
- Do you have to lie a lot to protect his feelings?
- Are you letting her take pictures of you in situations that make you feel uncomfortable just because you want her to like you?
- Does she threaten to hurt herself if you leave her?
- Does he threaten you or your family?
- Has she threatened to out you?
- Has he kept you from your friends or humiliated you in front of other people?
- Has she forced you to have sex when you didn't want to?

These are all signs of an abusive relationship. Abusive relationships can happen at any age and between any combinations of genders. If you think you're in an abusive relationship, you have to do everything in your power to leave. And we mean really leave. Abusers will apologize and promise to change until the cows come home. And for a while, they might be really good to you. But then the tension builds, and suddenly they strike out again. Then they say they're sorry, ask for your forgiveness, and treat you like a princess until they turn on you again. It's a pattern that will play itself out over and over again unless you stop it. It can be tempting to stay in an abusive relationship for the "good" times, but once the relationship has devolved to the point of physical or emotional violence, it has practically no chance of ever righting itself again.

If you see yourself in any of these situations, find someone you can trust—whether it be a friend, a therapist, or a relative—and tell him or her what's happening.

Remember that breaking up with an abusive partner can be particularly dangerous because the person is upset and angry that you're leaving. Make sure you have the support of friends and family to keep you safe, whether it's letting them know ahead of time that you're planning to break up with your boyfriend or girlfriend or actually bringing someone with you when you do it. And if you ever feel like you're in immediate danger, don't hesitate to call the police.

For further help, call the National Domestic Violence Hotline (800-799-SAFE) for resources in your area.

BREAKING UP

Oof! What once seemed like a pot of gold now smells like week-old gym socks. Your feelings have changed—it could be you, it could be your partner, it could just be fate—and you can't seem to get back to Wonderland. Maybe you're feeling held back by the relationship. Or maybe just the thought of having another hour-long conversation about how he wants the smallest dog in the world so it can fit inside his bejeweled cell phone holder makes you want to erase your online profiles, move to China, and disappear completely. Sorry, Charlie: not gonna happen. At some point, you're going to have to have to work up the courage to break it off.

If your feelings about someone change or if his behavior is making you more angry than happy, even after you've tried to talk about it, then you need to be honest with yourself and with him and move on. Staying with someone or being dishonest about your feelings just because you're afraid that you'll never find anything better is selling yourself short, plain and simple. And if you're not in love with him any longer but you're staying in the relationship because you're afraid of hurting him—well, that isn't doing either of you any favors. Maybe you'll wrestle with it for a while and try to fix everything, maybe you'll go through an exhausting cycle of break-up-and-make-up. But eventually you'll have to grit your teeth and rip off the Scooby Doo Band-Aid.

How should you do it? Be direct, clear, and compassionate. And don't try to get your partner to do it for you. The worst thing you can do when you need to break up with someone is to act all cold and hope that he loses interest. You know: show up late for dinner, kiss him on the cheek instead of making out, only say "unh-huh" when you're supposed to be having a conversation. Passive-aggressive much? And if he doesn't get the hint, you'll just grow to dislike him even more because he's so clueless. You may finally get so fed up that you just blurt out a bunch of mean things. Now you've really hurt him and you also don't feel so good about yourself.

When you feel like it's time to get out of a relationship, just do it. You'll respect yourself a lot more, and he'll respect you more, too (though he might be too heart-broken to realize it at the time).

GOOD BREAKUP CONVERSATION STARTERS

If it's time to break up, you'll need to sit your soon-to-be ex down and have "the talk." It's never easy — in fact, it's one of the hardest things to do. But remember, you're doing this for the good of you both. The conversation doesn't have to get messy. You don't have to run down all the things that bug you about her or how she did everything wrong. If you're really ready to break up, none of that matters now; nothing she may offer to do is going to change your mind. So, just say what you need to say and try to keep it brief. Avoid dragging the situation out by saying things like, "I'll call you later" or setting a time when you can talk about it more. If you want to stay friends, it's fine to say that, but keep in mind that you probably won't be the first person she'll call to have a fun night on the town — at least not for a while. And be prepared for some raw emotion from her; no one likes to be broken up with, and people often cry or yell when it happens. Just try to stay calm.

On the next page are a few ways to start the breakup conversation. Obviously, every situation calls for its own unique way of handling it, but here are some common approaches. Remember to only use the words that honestly apply to your situation (i.e., don't say you want to be friends if you don't want to).

- *"I've really enjoyed the good times we've shared together, but I feel it's time for both of us to move on."*

- *"It's been awesome hanging out with you, but I've realized that I like you more as a friend than romantically."*

- *"I wanted to talk to you because I don't think this relationship is going well for either of us anymore."*

- *"Thank you for being such a great person in my life these past few [weeks, months, years], but my feelings have changed. I really care for you, but I think we should start hanging out in a different capacity."*

GETTING OVER IT

Sometimes you're the one that gets dumped. Unless it's mutual or you've suspected something for a while and thus had a little prep time, it can come as a shock. You may feel angry and hopeless. You may blame yourself and immediately think that you're no good or go over every minute you spent together, looking for clues as to what went wrong. Especially as a queer person, you may feel that you'll never meet anyone again, or that no one will ever want you. All we can tell you is that those thoughts pass through almost everyone's minds when they get dumped. Thankfully, they're not true. If they were, no one would ever have a second relationship!

IN MARKE'S WORDS

My Love Blunder

I always considered myself to be a romantic person—so much so that I thought my life would never be complete until I found Mr. Right. Every night I would imagine what he would be like and how he would sweep me off my feet and solve all my problems with a wave of his rough, manly hands. He would write amazing poetry! He would cook me gourmet Spanish meals! He would have perfect hair!

Finally I met someone who fit all my expectations. He seemed smarter than me, more together financially, and had a killer sense of style. I fell head over heels in love. But after two weeks, my phone stopped ringing. Whenever I'd call him, he'd act cold and say he'd get back to me. I was crushed. Finally, I confronted him about it. He told me that he just didn't find me to be that interesting.

Then it hit me. I'd been so focused on finding the perfect boyfriend that I hadn't been making myself the perfect boyfriend for someone else! I also realized that I'd gone from relationship to relationship, rejecting guys as soon as their behavior deviated from the script in my head. If he pronounced something on the menu wrong or listened to music that I didn't like or wore something on a date that didn't complement his eye color—bam! I'd toss him on the trash heap. I missed out on some great relationship opportunities by thinking that no one I went out with was just right. I'd become totally judgmental—and kind of mean.

After that, I took some time off from dating to make myself a more well-rounded person. I wrote my own poetry and tried to teach myself Spanish cooking. Even better, when I went back to dating, I was able to be more broad-minded and to accept people for who they were—not who I wanted them to be.

Still, it's horrible to feel that way. Getting dumped sucks. We've both been through it, and really, the only cure is time. We know that sounds ridiculous when you're in a state of despair or heartbreak. But it's true. You may find yourself obsessing about your ex. What is he doing now? Does she still have the Ariel Schrag books I gave her? Is he seeing someone else? These thoughts are normal, but try not to let them run your life. Definitely do not stalk your ex in any way, either online or in person. That can lead to legal trouble and will only hurt you more. Hiding behind a car, waiting for your ex to leave school is just plain creepy, even if you don't mean anything bad by it.

During times of desperation, it's easy to work yourself up into a panic or get hooked on feeling sorry for yourself. Listening to metalcore and reading gloomy poetry are fine and can help you feel connected to others who feel the same way, but don't take on Depressed-and-Miserable as your new identity. You don't want to miss out on the rest of your life over someone who wasn't ready for your fabulousness! After you've cried yourself to sleep for a couple of nights and felt sufficiently sorry for yourself, shake that beautiful hair of yours and get back to living. Remember to exercise, get out of the house, spend tons of time with your friends, and get creative with your emotions, whether you express yourself through journaling, making art, or playing music. Or do something totally wild and out of character, like learning to ride a horse, joining a water polo team, or actually cleaning out your closet. It will make you feel like a better, more together person. If you are really having trouble climbing out of your funk, see a counselor or therapist (more on page 52) or contact The Trevor Project or another one of the organizations in the Resources section. And always vow to grow from the experience. So what if some dork didn't get how great you are? That just means that someone else will: We promise. You're a truly unique and special person, with a ton of sexy potential. (It's true.)

Breakup Dos and Don'ts

Ready to break up? Here are a few words of wisdom to live by.

DO

- ⊚ Make sure you really want to break up. It's confusing and unfair to the other person if you are wishy-washy.

- ⊚ Say it in person.

- ⊚ Be kind. Be firm and clear, not cold and cruel.

- ⊚ Be efficient.

DON'T

- ⊚ Break up in a text message.

- ⊚ Break up on a public online space.

- ⊚ Break up in public where she can make a scene—unless you're afraid she might get violent.

- ⊚ Lie and tell him you just want to be alone if you've got someone else in the wings.

- ⊚ Let guilt take over. It's almost impossible to break up with someone without hurting his or her feelings, but if you allow yourself to be overcome with guilt, you might wind up back together—and have to do the whole thing again.

- ⊚ Draw it out. Say what you have to say, but don't stick around and process for hours.

SEVEN

THE BIG
"S"

QUEER SEX

All teens have questions about sex, but queer teens often have more. That's because no one is talking about queer sex at home, in health class, or even in the school bathrooms. This is not to say that queer sex is so different from straight sex—it's not. Queer people do it for most of the same reasons, and we face a lot of the same risks. The only difference is that what we consider to be sex and what straight people consider to be sex is sometimes different.

Queer sex is just as natural and healthy as straight sex. And it doesn't matter that queer sex doesn't lead to reproduction (in case you were worried about that). Lots of straight sex—oral and anal sex, vaginal sex with birth control—doesn't lead to reproduction either! The whole point of sex (even when it does lead to reproduction) is to enjoy each other's bodies. Queer sex is great, and there's nothing weird about it at all.

When's the right time to have sex? Often sex happens as a natural progression of an intimate relationship with your boyfriend or girlfriend. You get to know each other while dating and hanging out, and you gradually work your way up to being intimate together. Other times, sex can be more immediate. You meet someone and it happens quickly, based purely on physical attraction. Some people see sex as an expression of love, and others see it as a fun way to spend a few hours or to release some tension. And sometimes, especially when you're young, it's simply a matter of experimentation. You just want to know how everything works, how it all fits together, and what all the fuss is about.

All teens—queer or not—have one thing in common: You're at an age when sex is suddenly on your mind all the time. But just because everyone is thinking and talking about it, doesn't mean everyone is doing it. In fact, a 2007 study found fewer than half of high school students have had sex. So, if you aren't already doing it, you shouldn't feel like you need to start having sex this very minute. If you're not ready, don't worry—you'll get there when the time is right. If you think you are ready—or are already doing it—make sure you are informed about all of the risks involved so that you can be safe and protect yourself and your partner.

Sex can be a valuable, enlightening, and even spiritual experience if you know what you're getting yourself into and have the maturity to handle it.

ARE YOU READY?

How will you know if you're ready to have sex? Does a giant light bulb go on above your bed? Does a loud gong sound in the back of your mind? Unfortunately, no. (At least not that we know of!) The decision about whether or not to have sex is based on how you (and your partner) feel. Many people don't feel comfortable having sex until they fall in love. That's totally fine. Others want to have sex before then. That's fine, too. And some people simply choose not have sex, which is also a perfectly valid option. If you're like most teens, there's a good chance you feel conflicted when it comes to sex. Sometimes your mind says no but your body screams yes. Other times, your body may not feel ready for it, but your mind thinks it's the right thing to do. That's natural. Sex can be confusing, even for older people. If you can wait until both your mind and body agree on the matter, you'll probably be happier for it in the long run.

Most important, know the risks and protect yourself (more on that later in this chapter) and don't ever feel pressured to do anything you don't want to do. You own your own comfort zone. It's part of what makes you special and unique. Stick to your standards and never compromise just to please anyone else, even your boyfriend or girlfriend.

STARTING SOLO

Before you start having sex with someone else, you may want to have some with yourself. Apart from being fun and safe, masturbation is also a fantastic way to learn about your own body in terms of where and how you like to be touched. And because you're the only one involved, you'll rarely be disappointed! The fantasies you have while you're touching yourself can sometimes teach you a lot about yourself, too, by helping clue you in to what kinds of sexual activities you may want to explore with a partner. Of course, sometimes fantasies are just that: fantasies. So don't get all freaked out if the Dallas Cowboy cheerleaders pop up in your mind while you masturbate. You may not want to have sex with 20 cheerleaders in real life, but you might still like the fantasy. You might fantasize about straight sex occasionally—even if you're gay. Sometimes kids get freaked out about this and wonder if it means they're not really gay at all. Just remember that fantasies are one thing and reality is another.

While people often masturbate before they have sex for the first time, they don't stop masturbating just because they've started having sex with other people. Masturbation is different from having sex because you have no one else to be concerned with but your-self—and you can do it anytime you like and don't need anyone else's consent! (Although we do recommend that you do it in the privacy of your own room or bath-room.) Masturbation can be a healthy part of your sex life whether you're single, in a relationship, young, old, whatever. And despite the fact that people always seem embarrassed about it, it's nothing to be ashamed of. That doesn't mean you should go posting updates about it on your profile online. But you should know that it's normal and that pretty much everyone is doing it. Of course, if you don't feel the urge to masturbate, that's fine, too! You can play—or not play—with your body however you like.

WHAT DOES IT MEAN TO "LOSE IT"?

You might be wondering what it even means for you, as a queer person, to lose your virginity. The way straight kids usually see it, he sticks his penis in her vagina and voilà! They're both devirginated. But for queers, it can be a little more complicated. Sure, you lose your virginity the first time you have sex with another person. But how do queer people define sex? Is it oral sex? Penetration? Any kind of genital contact? Does a tongue have to be involved or do fingers count? The answer is: There is no answer. Or rather, it's up to you to come up with the answer. This is another great part of being queer: You get to decide what sex is to you. You also don't need to play into any pre-established gender roles regarding your sexuality. You get to make up all of your own rules.

YOUR FIRST TIME

TV, movies, and books often create a lot of mystique about losing your virginity. There's so much mystery, emotion, and build up about it. Some of it is real, and a bunch of it is just empty hype. But it is true that sharing your first time with someone special to you can often make you feel closer to them and bring back special memories later in your life.

What will your first time be like? Remember the first time you rode a bike or sang in public or tried to write a poem? You probably put in your best effort, but looking back, it wasn't perfect, was it? It's the same with sex. Your first time might be amazing, but chances are it will just be so-so. And that's OK. You wouldn't expect your

---

Not Doing It

We talked earlier about waiting for the right time to have sex – and we highly recommend it! It's always preferable to wait to have sex until you feel ready or find the right person, even if that means waiting a really long time. Also, some people (often referred to as *asexual*) actually never feel sexually attracted to other people, and they still lead full and healthy lives. (Many people, queer and straight, go through asexual periods in their lives, too, where they aren't interested in sex for a few months or even years.) It's your decision to have sex, and whenever it is, it's fine. Of course, if you've been sexually abused in your past and you think that might be hampering your desire to have sex now, you should seek counseling. See the Resources section for places to call.

first time playing the piano to win you a Grammy. The truth is that many people walk away from their first time saying, "That's it? That's what all the fuss was about?" This isn't to say they don't want to do it again; it just usually takes a little practice to find your sex groove.

Some people think that if you're gay or lesbian, sex will be easier because you know how everything works and will automatically know what to do. That's only a little true. We've both done it with people who could probably be mistaken for our twins, and we still wound up thinking, "Whoa, you're into that?" Everyone's body is different, and that means a different sexual experience with each person, each time you do it. Sex is an expression of one's personality—it's part of who you are—and that is what makes each relationship and encounter unique.

Will Sex Affirm My Queerness?

As we talked about in Chapter 1, some people think they need to have queer sex to be sure they are queer, but it's not true. You'll know you're queer by what you feel inside and by who you feel attracted to—not by what you do when you're naked. Lots of people know they are queer from the time they are very young—like 10 years old—and you can be sure they aren't having a lot of sex then! Doing it with someone of the same sex doesn't prove someone is homosexual or bisexual. Wanting to be with them or simply imagining a happy life together would be better indicators. Don't have sex to prove anything to yourself or to the world. There are lots of valid reasons to do it, but that's not one of them.

DOING IT

Just as there are many different types of relationships, there are a gazillion ways to have sex. Not all gay men have anal sex, nor do all lesbians like oral sex. It's a rainbow, darling. You'll need to figure out for yourself what you like. That's why at some point it's important to find a partner with whom you feel comfortable experimenting to see what feels right to you. And learn to listen to your partner and pay attention to how he or she responds to certain things—remember, it's not all about you. Talking about sex with a regular partner can help you refine your technique. It may seem awkward at first to talk about it, but it can lead to better sex, so it's worth it. Also, have patience. You may need some practice to become comfortable with sharing your body with someone else. Very few people say no to the opportunity for more practice!

So what is queer sex? Anything you want it to be! Here are a few ways queer people have sex.

⊚ **Touching and rubbing.** Genital stimulation can come from any body part. You can use your hands or hips or feet, or you can rub your private parts on someone's thigh, arm, butt, genitals, ankles, wherever. (This is called *tribadism* when women do it and *frotting* when men do it.) You may stroke his penis, insert fingers into his anus, or insert fingers into her vagina. The latter two may also be considered anal and vaginal sex, respectively. You may find yourself making out, getting all hot and heavy, and having an orgasm just from rubbing against each other's bodies. You may not even have to take your clothes off! It's all sex, it feels really good, and the best part is there is a decreased risk of spreading sexually transmitted infections (STIs, see page 169) when all you do is touch and rub. If you are inserting fingers into somewhere, you may want consider using a rubber glove to help prevent the spread of diseases like syphilis, which is on the rise among gay men.

⊚ **Oral sex.** Oral sex is when you put your mouth on your partner's genitals. For guys it's called *fellatio* or "giving him a blow job." For girls, it's called *cunnilingus* or "going down on her." There's no one way for oral because everyone likes something different. Using your tongue is usually a good thing. Teeth, not so much. The best person to give you feedback is your partner. Using a condom with guys or a dental dam with girls during oral sex helps prevent the transmission of STIs.

◎ **Anal sex.** Any kind of penetrating sexual activity involving the anus is typically called anal sex. This can involve penetration with the penis, fingers, or a sex toy. STIs like HIV and hepatitis B spread more easily through anal sex than via oral sex or rubbing. Be sure to always use a condom and plenty of lubricant when engaging in any kind of anal penetration, as the anus does not lubricate itself (see more on page 177). Also, never insert a finger, toy, or penis into any body part after it's been in a butthole without thoroughly washing it. The anus has a lot of bacteria that, when spread elsewhere, can cause lots of problems. Sex toys for anal penetration made of silicone are best because, as long as they don't have electrical components, they can be easily cleaned and disinfected. Just boil them in hot water for five minutes or run them through the dishwasher. (Make sure they cool off before you use them again!) Or better yet, use a fresh condom on the toy each time. Penetrating the anus with other foreign objects like food can be dangerous, so don't do it—even if it seems like a good idea at the moment. With any kind of anal sex, go slow, remember to use plenty of lube, and stop if something doesn't feel comfortable. Sex should feel good. It shouldn't hurt.

◎ **Vaginal sex.** This is when a penis, finger, or sex toy is inserted into a vagina. Some lesbians enjoy vaginal sex with dildos—faux penises that are often made from silicone or rubber—or other types of toys, like battery-powered vibrators. As mentioned above, dildos made of silicone are best because they can be most easily cleaned. Condoms can also be used to keep the toys clean. In most places you can't buy sex toys until you are 18, so if you're under 18, toys might not be an option. Some bisexual people have vagina-penis sex just the way straight kids do. And some trans kids have it, too. Lots of gay male kids experiment with vaginal sex as well to see if they like it. Anytime a penis and vagina are involved in vaginal sex, unintended pregnancy can happen, so be sure to use condoms to prevent pregnancy—and STIs.

RAISE THE RAINBOW FLAG

Ever wonder how the rainbow flag became our symbol? San Francisco artist Gilbert Baker was looking for a colorful and optimistic symbol to represent the new atmosphere of gay freedom, visibility, and diversity in the 1970s. He came up with the rainbow design. In 1978, he and 30 volunteers hand-dyed and stitched prototypes of the rainbow flag and flew them in the Gay Freedom Day parade (as Gay Pride Day was then called) in June. When Harvey Milk was assassinated later that same year, the community rallied behind the flag, and it was adopted as the official emblem of San Francisco's 1979 Gay Pride parade. Along with the pink triangle and the Greek letter lambda, the rainbow is now an internationally recognized symbol for queerness.

SEXUALLY TRANSMITTED INFECTIONS

Everything you do in life comes with potential risks, sex included. So if you think you're ready to have sex, make sure you are ready to protect yourself against STIs. These are viral and bacterial infections that are transmitted via bodily fluids like blood, semen, and vaginal secretions as well as through skin contact of the genitals. They include infections like HIV, syphilis, herpes, hepatitis, gonorrhea, and HPV.

You should take sexually transmitted infections very seriously; they can cause extreme emotional and physical pain and, in some cases, death. But as long as you educate yourself about the risks and practice safer sex to help avoid them, you'll be able to engage in sex responsibly. And contrary to popular belief, safe sex is important for lesbians, too! Girls can also carry STIs and need to be just as responsible for engaging in safer behaviors. You can find out more online at the Centers for Disease Control and Prevention (cdc.gov/std).

STI or STD?

In recent years, doctors started referring to STDs (sexually transmitted diseases) as STIs (sexually transmitted infections) because they wanted to drive home the fact that you can still be infected even if you have no symptoms. People tend to think that they don't have a disease if there is nothing obviously wrong with them, but your partner can be infected even if he or she looks totally healthy—and so can you. When talking about STIs/STDs, it's fine to use either expression.

KNOW THE FACTS

Here's a rundown of some basic STIs, what they do, how you contract them, and what the treatment is for them.

DISEASE	HOW YOU GET IT	SYMPTOMS	TESTS	TREATMENT
Herpes Simplex Virus I and II (HSV I and II)	Skin-to-skin contact during vaginal, anal, or oral sex or during sexual activities in which you rub exposed skin together.	HSV I (a.k.a. cold sores) typically appears on the mouth, and HSV II typically appears on the genitals, though both can be present in either place. If you have HSV on the mouth, you'll get cold sores from time to time during an outbreak. If you've been exposed to genital herpes, you'll most likely notice genital itching or pain, followed by painful sores about 2 to 20 days after being infected. You may also have painful urination, fever, and headaches. However, some people who get the virus don't have any symptoms at all, so it's important to remember that you may still be infected (and contagious) without any symptoms.	Skin swab of infected area or blood test.	There is no cure for herpes, so once you have it, you have it for life. It can be treated with an antiviral medication, however, that will lessen the frequency and length of outbreaks and reduce the chance of spreading it to others.
Human Papillomavirus (HPV)	Skin-to-skin contact during vaginal, oral, or anal sex.	HPV is a virus (with more than 100 strains) that causes abnormal cell growth in the cervix. It can lead to genital warts and even, in some cases, cancer. For girls, the warts are on or near the vulva, vagina, cervix, or anus. In guys, they are near or on the penis, scrotum, or anus. Warts can be any size, are usually whitish or flesh-colored, and are sometimes hard to see. You can also be infected with HPV and not have genital warts; in this case, it is still possible to pass the virus along to someone else, who can get the symptoms.	Swab test of the cervix for women (also known as a Pap smear). There is not a test for men.	Usually the body will cure the infection in one or two years, but for those who get secondary medical problems such as warts or cancer, those things have to be treated more aggressively. There is a fairly new vaccination recommended for females between the ages of 9 and 26 that is effective at preventing certain strains of the virus, so do ask your doctor about this.

DISEASE	HOW YOU GET IT	SYMPTOMS	TESTS	TREATMENT
Human Immuno- deficiency Virus/ Auto Immune Deficiency Syndrome (HIV/ AIDS)	Exchange of body fluids mainly through vaginal and anal sex and, in very rare cases, oral sex. When only the virus is present, some- one is considered HIV positive; after symptoms start to present themselves, the patient is con- sidered to have AIDS.	Symptoms usually do not occur for seven to ten years, which makes it very easy for someone to spread HIV with- out knowing it. The virus af- fects the immune system by destroying the defense cells that fight infectious diseases in the body. People with HIV get serious infections they normally wouldn't get. Com- mon symptoms are recurring infections throughout the body as well as weight loss, chronic diarrhea, white spots in the mouth, fever, fatigue, vaginal infections, growths and open sores on the skin, and night sweats.	Blood test or mouth swab.	There is no cure for HIV/AIDS, but there are antiviral medica- tions that can boost the immune system and prolong the life of the infected person, even allowing them to have an active and enjoyable lifestyle, as long as they are willing to follow all precautions to remain healthy. However, the drugs can have very severe side effects. Also, after years of treatment with antiviral medications, the disease may become resistant to them, resulting in large-scale infections and illnesses, which eventually lead to death. The fact that HIV/AIDS is not cur- able is why prevention is so important.
Thri- chomo- niasis	Exchange of body fluids during penis-to-vagina or vulva-to-vulva sex.	It is caused by a little parasite that usually lives in the vagina (in women) and in the urethra (in men). The symptoms usually show up within 5-28 days of being exposed to an infected person and include slight burning after urination, foamy vaginal discharge, and itching and burning in the vagina.	Swab test of the vagina or of secre- tions from the penis.	Prescription medications.

DISEASE	HOW YOU GET IT	SYMPTOMS	TESTS	TREATMENT
Chlamydia	Exchange of bodily fluids during vaginal, anal, or oral sex.	Like gonorrhea, chlamydia is caused by bacteria. It's one of the most common STIs because 75% of women and 50% of men show no symptoms (and spread it unknowingly). When symptoms are present they usually show up 1 to 3 weeks after exposure, and they include painful urination; abdominal cramping especially during sex; itchy or swollen testicles; and genital discharge.	Urine test or swab test of the mouth, anus, cervix, or urethra. In men, a urine test or swab test taken from the opening of the urethra.	Antibiotics. If untreated, chlamydia can lead to pelvic inflammatory disease (PID), sterility, or infertility.
Pubic Lice (Crabs)	Skin-to-skin (or really, hair-to-hair) contact during sexual activity. Just like head lice, crabs can also live in fabrics, making it possible to catch them from someone's infested clothing, towel, or bedding. If you are within their proximity, they will jump onto you.	Pubic lice are tiny insects that live by sucking blood from their host (you), causing itching and a presence of eggs and bugs in pubic hair. You'll start to notice symptoms usually within a 1-3 weeks.	Just by looking. Pubic lice look like small flakes of skin, and their eggs look like grey or white dots that hold onto strands of pubic hair.	There are special lice-killing shampoos specifically for crabs that should take care of the bugs on your body, but you'll also need to dry clean all your bedding, towels, and clothing to kill all the lice and their eggs.
Gonorrhea	Exchange of body fluids during vaginal, anal, or oral sex.	A bacterium that grows and multiplies in the warm, moist areas of the reproductive tract in both girls and guys, resulting in painful urination, smelly discharge, fever, and severe abdominal pain. It can also lead to sterility or the inability to reproduce. The same bacterium can grow in your mouth, throat, eyes, and anus.	Swab test of the mouth, anus, vagina, cervix, urethra or the discharge from the penis.	Antibiotics.

DISEASE	HOW YOU GET IT	SYMPTOMS	TESTS	TREATMENT
Syphilis	Skin-to-skin contact during vaginal, anal, or oral sex as well as from rubbing rubbing genitals together.	It starts with painless sores (in the spot where the contact was made with the infected person's body) ten days to three months after sexual contact. Sometimes there are sores inside the anus or vagina that go un-noticed. Three weeks to six months after contact, there can be flulike illness with rashes. If untreated, syphilis can eventually lead to blind-ness, brain deterioration, shooting pains in the limbs, loss of feeling in parts of the body, damage to the organs, and even death.	Swab test on areas with vis-ible open sores (penis, vagina, anus), or blood test. If more advanced, spinal fluid test.	Antibiotics. But if left untreated, some of the damage to the body may be irreversible.
Scabies	Skin-to-skin contact during sexual activity. (Scabies is not solely an STI; it can also be contracted by coming into contact with in-fected clothing or bedding.)	Scabies occurs when very small insects called mites burrow into the skin, lay eggs, and produce secretions that cause a rash of small red bumps and blisters. It is most likely to show up on the waist, knees, webs of fingers, genitals, and elbows first but will eventually cover the whole body.	Medical examina-tion of the skin.	Medicated soap and decontamination of all bedding and clothing.

STI chart courtesy of Nikol Hasler, and is taken from her book *Sex: A Book For Teens*.

SAFER SEX

Though most people use the term "safe sex," it's more correct to say "safer sex" because no sex is 100 percent safe. That being said, using protection goes a long way toward protecting you against STIs. Below are explanations of the best forms of protection and instructions on how to use them.

Condoms. A condom, or rubber, is a shield for the penis that is usually made of latex (although there are polyurethane ones for people who are allergic to latex). It helps prevent the exchange of semen (cum), blood, or other body fluids from one partner to another. It is the best way to prevent the transmission of HIV and other STIs. Always use a condom for anal or vaginal sex that involves a penis. Using a condom for oral sex with a penis also helps protect against many STIs, such as herpes, which can be transferred from the mouth to the genitals (and vice versa) pretty easily. Be sure to store condoms in a cool, dry place because exposure to heat can break down the latex.

To use:

1. Check the expiration date.

2. Unwrap it carefully. If you tear the package apart in the heat of the moment, you might also tear the condom. Uh oh.

3. Gently squeeze the air out of the condom tip, which is a receptacle for semen, before placing it on the head of the penis and slowly rolling it down toward the base.

4. Apply plenty of water-based lubricant on the outside of the condom and on the area to be penetrated before engaging in anal or vaginal sex. (Oil-based lubricants can damage the condom.) This is even more important for anal sex because, while the vagina lubricates itself to make it ready for sex, the anus does not.

5. Check to make sure the condom is still on securely if you change positions or if you're having sex for a long time. It's OK to take a break to make sure the condom is still on.

6. Hold the condom tightly at the base when withdrawing from a body cavity.

7. Throw the condom in the trash after it's been used. Never use the same condom twice. It's unsafe and also kind of gross.

Dental dams. A dental dam is a square or rectangular piece of latex that can be used during oral sex to protect against the transmission of skin-to-skin STIs, like herpes. To use, you hold the dental dam in place over the vagina or anus before having oral sex. This way, the mouth doesn't actually come into contact with the genitals. (If you want to use lubrication, put a dollop of it on the body part before putting the dam in place.) Make sure to make some kind of mark on one side to remind you which side is facing up. This will prevent you from accidentally flipping it over.

Gloves. Most STIs cannot be passed from finger to genitals, but some—like syphilis—can. If you want to be safe, use a latex gloves when you finger someone or they finger you. Lubricate the outside of the glove with a water-based lube before inserting it into someone. Latex gloves can also be used as dental dams if you cut them open and cut off the middle three fingers.

OTHER TIPS FOR CLEANLINESS AND SAFETY

Keep sex toys clean. If you use sex toys like dildos or vibrators, use condoms with them or wash them carefully after use. If they are made of silicone, just boil them in water for five minutes or run them through the dishwasher.

Keep your hands clean. Always wash your hands before and after sex if you're fingering someone, and keep your nails short to avoid any cuts.

Keep your parts clean. Finally, you don't have to rub yourself down with alcohol (that would irritate the bejesus out of your genitals), but do keep your penis or vagina and anus clean. It will help prevent the spread of bacteria during sex.

What Is Lubrication?

Lubrication, or *lube* for short, is used to make sex go smoother. Women produce vaginal lubrication when turned on, but sometimes adding a little extra can lessen friction and irritation during sex. Fingers and toys will glide in and out more easily if you use lube. Since the anus doesn't provide any natural lubrication, lube is essential for any kind of anal penetration. If you are using latex protection, such as a condom or dental dam, be sure to use a water-based or silicone lubricant. Oil-based lubes will break down the latex. Most people don't use lube for oral sex, but if you do, don't use lube that contains any kind of chemicals, such as nonoxynol-9.

IN KATHY'S WORDS

My One-Night Stand

I was 19 and had been out for about a year when I made a trip to San Francisco with two friends. We'd heard that San Francisco was a gay Mecca, and we wanted to see it for ourselves. On the drive out, my two friends got closer and closer, and by the time we reached the Bay Area, they were all hot and heavy for each other, and I was starting to feel like a third wheel.

We went out to a lesbian bar, and this cute woman, Debra, was hitting on me. I'd never had a one-night stand before, and since the friends I came with were hooking up, I decided, "Why not?" The only problem was that I was pretty inexperienced. Although I'd dated a couple of girls, neither had been serious relationships, and we'd never gotten very far.

So when I got to Debra's home, I suddenly got nervous. What would she want? Would I make a fool of myself for not knowing what to do? What if I don't touch her right and I'm exposed as the amateur that I am?

As we made our way to her bedroom, I could feel myself trembling. Debra must have sensed what was going on because she took my hand, looked me in the eye, and said, "We don't have to do anything you're not comfortable with." It turned out to be a very sweet, gentle experience.

It was then that I realized that we're not born knowing what to do in bed, and sexual inexperience is nothing to be ashamed of. Everyone needs to start somewhere!

SEX AND LOVE

One of the best things in the world can be having sex with someone you love. But when you're young, you're still figuring out both sex and love, so it can get a bit confusing. Is it love that you feel for her? Or is it just intense attraction? Do you really want to go steady with that guy? Or do you simply like what he does with his tongue? Because sex is so intimate, you can mistake it for love, which can lead to trouble.

For some teens, love is an absolute prerequisite to having sex, and they are willing to wait until they fall in love — or something that feels like love — to have sex. That way, they can feel like they're sharing an intimate part of themselves when the time is right. Other teens are OK with having sex without being in love, which is fine, so long as the sex is safe and respectful.

But for other teens, sex and love feel totally separate. They don't want to do all those hot, sexy things they fantasize about with someone as sweet and innocent as the person they have a crush on. If that's you, you might want to think about why that is and try to shift your thinking. We're not saying you need to be in love to have sex, but if you can only imagine having sex with someone you're *not* in love with, you might be seeing sex as something dirty or weird that can pollute your partner, and it's not. It's true that sex can seem scary, as if it has a mind of its own. But when sex is an honest, loving, safe experience, it's a beautiful thing to share with someone you love.

IN MARKE'S WORDS

Hold On, Bro

One night I was out with my friends, and I met this gorgeous guy who seemed really into me. He said all the right things and basically had me swooning in no time.

He took me somewhere private, and we started making out. Things started going fast—maybe a bit too fast. Before I knew it, we had torn each others' clothes off. Our bodies seemed to have minds of their own, and we were both caught up in it all. It looked like we were about to go all the way.

But, when the time came to do the deed, Mr. Wonderful said he didn't use condoms. For a minute, I thought I was just going to forget the consequences and do it anyway. One time couldn't hurt, right? And I was afraid of hurting his feelings and ruining the moment by telling him to stop.

But something in the back of my mind said, "No way!" I knew people who were living with HIV and other people who had gotten STIs, and I didn't want to have to go through what they were going through. Also, why was I worried about hurting the feelings of someone who was willing to put my life at risk? I hardly even knew this dude!

It took enormous willpower, but I told him to stop. I said it gently but firmly and told him that we could do other stuff instead. I never actually said, "Not without a rubber, buddy," but just redirected his attention to other activities. He seemed a little disappointed, but soon we were going at it safely. Looking back, I've never once regretted protecting myself that night. It just wasn't worth the risk.

ALL FOR ONE OR ONE FOR ALL?

If you do start to enter into a sexual relationship with someone, certain things need to be decided, like whether or not you will be exclusive. As we mentioned in Chapter 6, monogamy is having only one sexual partner, and some people are most comfortable in that situation. From a sexual perspective, the positive side to having a monogamous relationship is that you are at less risk for catching a disease when you only have one partner. (Fewer partners always means lower risk, even if you are using protection, which you should be.) Some people also feel closer to a partner when they know that he or she is not messing around with anyone else. However, some people don't like the idea of only being sexual with one other person because it feels too limiting to them. Those people will choose to have an open relationship, in which they are free to date or have sex with other partners. Either option is OK, as long as everyone involved agrees to it. Both types of sexual relationships require good communication and trust from all involved. And remember: It's best to be honest with yourself. If you know you can't be monogamous, don't enter into a relationship with someone for whom monogamy is important, or vice versa. That scene will just lead to a lot of hurt for everyone involved.

YOU LIKE TO DO WHAT?

Exploration is a big part of sex, and you might find that you're into some weird stuff. (Although if you only knew how many people were into "weird" stuff, you'd realize it's not so weird!) Some people like to role play (pretend to act like someone or something else during sex), dress up like animals, tie each other up, or wear leather and high heels. Hey, whatever makes your toes tingle! Just make sure that you don't take things too far and end up hurting yourself or the person you're with. Playing with ropes, knives, or other potentially dangerous objects can cause serious injury. And role-playing, if it gets out of hand or becomes an end unto itself, may cause psychological or emotional stress to the other person if he or she doesn't understand what's going on. Always talk about these situations first with your partner before you engage in them.

WHAT ABOUT PORN?

Sure, you're supposed to be over 18 to look at porn, but we know that lots of kids see it before then. In some places, it's the only exposure to queer sex that you can get. Curiosity is healthy, but don't confuse porn with information. First of all, no one has a body like a porn star, sometimes not even porn stars. (Hello, Photoshop, wide-angle lenses, and expensive wax jobs!) Sex on screen or in photos is not the same as in the real world, nor should it be. On screen, it's supposed to be a fantasy, full of tricks to make it seem more exciting. As a matter of fact, most "lesbian" porn is made by straight men for straight men and has very little to do with the way real lesbians have sex. Most gay porn is also often targeted toward a very specific audience. Porn is a business, and it's all about making money, honey — so don't start thinking it's based on any kind of reality. As we said earlier, there's no "true way" to have sex. You should just be yourself. If you act like a porn star during sex, you might as well be a robot. You also might as well be a comedian because your partner is probably going to start laughing. Just have fun when you're having sex. There's no need to perform because (thankfully!) you're not on camera. (And remember that if you're under 18, it's seriously illegal to be naked, let alone have sex, on camera.)

Size Doesn't Matter

Right now, society puts a lot of emphasis on unrealistic bodies. Impossibly skinny chicks with big boobs fill the pages of magazines. Macho dudes brag online about how big their penises are. But despite everything you've heard, the human body is beautiful in its many, varied forms. Everyone is unique, and different people are attracted to different things. For some, penis size doesn't matter. Others are turned on by a huge member. Some think large breasts are important. Others like them small. Whether you're thin, tall, hairy, busty, or have a big nose, some people will find you attractive and some won't. What matters is that you are a wonderful person with a lot of love and pleasure to give. If people can't see you for your true self, then screw them! (Well, not literally.)

SEX AND TECHNOLOGY

You probably spend a lot of your socializing time using some form of technology. It's cool to meet (and flirt with) other queer kids on the web, and it may even be necessary if there aren't a whole lot of other queer kids in your high school or town. The web is also great for connecting with other people in the local and international queer community, and it can give you an opportunity to meet queer adults who can offer support and encouragement. And everyone loves to communicate with friends and crushes via text. But just like your real-world life, your technological life can get complicated. Here are some things to remember as you cruise the queer sphere of technology.

◎ **Protect yourself.** There are a lot of weirdos online who might try to take advantage of you. They might say they want to befriend you but end up stealing your identity or money. Or they might want to meet you and force you to do stuff sexually that you don't want to do. Never give out your phone number or home address, and definitely do not send pictures of yourself naked. Set your profile to private and confirm your friends' identities on chat so you can be sure that you always know whom you are talking to.

◎ **Don't lie.** While you should never fully disclose your identity, phone number, or address when you first meet people online, that doesn't mean you should make up stuff. Telling someone that you're older or that you're going to meet them when you're really not is just wrong. (Remember, they're also queer and taking a chance by reaching out.) Also, the people you're fooling could get pissed off when they find out you've been lying and try to get revenge. So do everyone a favor and don't make stuff up.

◎ **Don't gossip or brag.** Sex is fun, but that doesn't mean it's a joke. Bragging about who you had sex with on Facebook to sound cool doesn't win you points; it only makes you look insecure. Gossiping about other peoples' sex lives can really hurt them, whether the stories you're spreading are true or not. That includes spreading rumors about STIs. And don't post about how you always want sex or brag about how much you like it. No one cares, and it can make you sound … kind of desperate.

◉ **Don't cruise for porn.** You can clear your cache and empty your trash all you want, but it's still possible for someone else to find a record of every website you've been to, every IM conversation you've had, and every image you've viewed on your computer. Nothing is ever really deleted. Your parents may not know how to do it, but if they wanted to find out, they could ask someone else to check. Most libraries and schools independently monitor what you're looking at on their computers as well. You thought tripping down the stairs last year was embarrassing. Try getting found out for watching porn flicks during study hall.

⊚ **Never post naked pictures.** In many states, putting up naked pictures of yourself or any other minor online counts as child pornography, and anyone who posts or views them—including yourself—can be arrested. Don't think that no one will catch you— entire police departments are dedicated to catching child pornographers. And just because everyone is doing it doesn't mean you won't be the one to get caught and get into trouble. As we said before, once online, always online. Those pictures can follow you around for the rest of your life or fall into the wrong hands and jeopardize your future. Imagine getting rejected from college or a sports team because of one bad decision you made.

⊚ **No sexting.** You've been dating your boyfriend for quite some time. You've seen each other naked. No big deal. One morning you wake up with a massive hard on and it makes you think of him. You grab your phone, snap a picture, and send it to him. Shouldn't be a problem, right? Wrong. We know it's tempting, and you probably look great naked on an iPhone screen. But it's illegal to have nude pictures of a minor on a hard drive, even if it's owned by another teen, so you could both get into trouble. And if you break up, do you really want naked pics of you floating around for everyone to see, especially if you're making your sexy but embarrassing "O" face? We didn't think so.

◉ **No private meet-ups with strangers.** It can be tempting to want to meet up with someone you met online, whether as a friend, a date, or even an anonymous sexual hookup. But don't ever go alone to meet up with a stranger you met online. There are lots of people who pretend to be one person and turn out to be another. Or sometimes they are exactly who they said they are—but are also criminally insane or want to force you into doing something you don't want to do. If you want to meet someone you met online, do it in a very public place and bring along friends. And if you were hoping to have some anonymous sex with a stranger, let that idea go. While blowing some kid you met online behind the 7-Eleven might seem like a good idea if you feel desperate and alone, it is probably going to make you feel worse than if you just hung out with friends or fantasized in your own bedroom. And if he turns out to be older and creepy, you could be putting yourself in real danger.

BAD SEX

Yes indeed: There is such a thing as bad sex—even with someone you love. It may not be mind-blowing every time. You may do things that you're not particularly into but that really turn your partner on. (Although that's not really bad sex; that's just a compromise.) You might be really hot for someone, but when it finally comes down to it, something just doesn't click and the whole thing fizzles out like a flat Pepsi.

Maybe you're having an awesome time, and then suddenly she says something that totally kills the mood. Or maybe you've been with someone awhile, and your sex life with them is starting to get stale. Just like relationships, sex involves some work. Sometimes you have to take the bad with the good or push yourself to try new things to keep it fresh. And sometimes you just have to know when to fold 'em and walk away. The chemistry isn't always there, and that's nobody's fault.

Don't Be Jailbait

If someone seriously older than you is asking for sex, think twice. For one, there's a possibility that he or she is trying to take advantage of you (see page 129). Also it's illegal for adults to have sex with minors, which means he or she could go to jail for being involved with you. There are legal repercussions for minors, as well. The legal ages for what is permissible vary from state to state, so check the rules in yours. And make sure that you are honest about your own age even if you are interested in someone older because you can get them in big trouble if you lie. If someone really cares about you, he or she will wait until you're a legal adult.

CONCLUSION

When we were growing up—which wasn't even that long ago—being LGBT was a totally different experience than it is now. There were way fewer role models, and homosexuality was rarely discussed, except when people were talking about AIDS or "sins of morality." Suffice it to say, it was not the most exciting time to be queer. We had to work hard to find queer comrades and really search for representations of LGBT people in books, art, and music. There weren't many.

And that was just a half-generation or so ago. Before that, it was even worse. It used to be illegal for queer people to express their affection in public, have sex, or dress the way they wanted. There was even a time when we could have been arrested for writing this book! But things are way different today. There are famous queer television and movie stars, out political and religious leaders, and a flood of books and web information. And both of us have been able to live openly, enter into loving queer relationships, advocate for full equality, and do what we love without fear of recrimination. We couldn't have done it without the bravery and truthfulness of other queer people, and we're hoping to inspire you to continue the legacy.

Now is a really exciting time to be queer because change is happening so rapidly. You may even see a difference in your school's attitude toward queer kids from the time you enter as a freshman to the time you graduate as a senior. (You may even be a part of making that change.) Lots of teens are already able to take same-sex dates to prom. Perhaps you are one of them. Maybe you are out to your parents or have a boyfriend or girlfriend who you can hold hands with at the movies. Maybe you're trans and have found a loving group of friends who accept you for who you are. Don't take this stuff for granted. Queer teens and their supporters have fought hard for these things, and while the fight for queer rights and acceptance isn't over by a long shot, every baby step of visibility, honesty, and activism gets us a little closer to full equality. It's no longer a pipe dream to be out and to live a normal life in this country. It's a near-reality, and it's up to you to keep pressing ahead to make it happen.

So what to do? Reading this book is a great start. The next thing to do—if you haven't already—is to educate yourself and to connect to the larger queer community. There are thousands of other queer people going through the same things that you are. You just need to find one another. You'll probably encounter some pretty sizeable hurdles in your quest to be free or to find out more about yourself, but it'll be easier to overcome them if you know where to go for help, support, and empowerment. The resources on the following page should get you started and hopefully will inspire you to live your life on your own terms: out, proud, and free.

RESOURCES

QUEER ORGANIZATIONS

Become a part of the global queer community! The organizations below will help you connect with others, get up-to-date info on queer issues, and offer a hand when you need one.

About.com: GLBT Teens
gayteens.about.com
This is a great place to learn about issues of importance to LGBT teens, from coming out to getting involved in your community to sharing about dating and sex.

About.com: Lesbian Life
lesbianlife.about.com
Find information about everything, from lesbian celebrities to queer politics to dating, sex, and marriage.

About.com: Gay Life
gaylife.about.com
Get advice and information from a gay man's perspective about health, love, sex, relationships, and more.

Lavender Youth Recreation & Information Center (LYRIC)
in San Francisco
lyric.org
The website for San Francisco's LGBT youth resource center has lots of good info.

Queer Attitude: LGBT Teen and Global Gay Youth Community
queerattitude.com
Forums, photo galleries, and blogs by and for LGBT youth can be found on this website.

The Gay Youth Corner (GYC)
thegyc.com
Three different queer youth chat rooms offer you opportunities to get advice, chill out, or debate an issue.

PlanetOut
planetout.com
One of the first queer websites, PlanetOut is a place to catch up on celebrity gossip with a queer sensibility.

Trans Youth
transyouth.com
This site specifically for transgender, non-gender-conforming youth, and their friends has info on surgeries, dating, sex, trans pride, and almost everything else you might want to know.

Advocates for Youth
advocatesforyouth.org
Find LGBT-friendly sexual health information for youths.

The Trevor Project
thetrevorproject.org
This is a 24-hour suicide help line and support resource for LGBT teens. Call 1-866-4-U-Trevor or visit the website.

The GLBT National Help Center
glnh.org
Volunteers staff the youth talk line at this website that provides help and resources for LGBT and questioning individuals in times of need. Call 1-800-246-PRIDE or visit the website.

The Gay, Lesbian, and Straight Education Network (GLSEN)
glsen.org
Find resources for teens in school, including info on the Day of Silence and how to start a Gay-Straight Alliance in your school.

PFLAG: Parents, Families, and Friends of Lesbians and Gays
pflag.org
This is a resource for people who love people who are queer.

Center Link
lgbtcenters.org
This group is an organization for LGBT community centers.

Its website is a great place to get involved in the LGBT community, learn about different programs, and locate the community center nearest you.

QUEER RELIGIOUS WEBSITES

Many organized religions have members who want to reach out to the LGBT community. Check out these websites for their perspectives.

CHRISTIAN

Whosoever
whosoever.org
This online magazine has information and discussion groups about what it means to be queer and Christian.

Gay Church
gaychurch.org
This site has a directory of LGBT-friendly churches, Bible discussion forums, and interpretations of what the Bible says about homosexuality.

HINDU

The Gay and Lesbian Vaishnava Association, Inc.
galva108.org
This site talks about the inclusivity of Hindu teachings.

JEWISH

The World Congress of Gay, Lesbian, Bisexual, and Transgender Jews: Keshet Ga'avah
glbtjews.org
Find connections and information about LGBT Jewish organizations around the world.

QUAKER
Friends for Lesbian, Gay, Bisexual, Transgender, and Queer Concerns
flgbtqc.quaker.org
Find out about the biannual Queer Quaker gathering, meet other Queer Quakers, and even share recipes!

SEVENTH-DAY ADVENTIST
Seventh-day Adventist Kinship
sdakinship.net
This website helps LGBT Adventists reconcile their religion with their sexual orientation or gender identity.

MORMON
Affirmation: Gay & Lesbian Mormons
affirmation.org
This site has support and information for gay, lesbian, bisexual, and transgender LDS and their family and friends.

QUEER BOOKS
Reading is a great way to get more in touch with queer life. Here are some of our favorite books.

RELIGIOUS
What the Bible Really Says About Homosexuality
by Daniel A. Helminiak

Jesus, The Bible, and Homosexuality: Explode the Myths, Heal the Church
by Jack Rogers

Bulletproof Faith: A Spiritual Survival Guide for Gay and Lesbian Christians
by Candace Chellew-Hodge

Stranger at the Gate: To Be Gay and Christian in America
by Mel White

RESOURCE

Gay-Straight Alliances: A Handbook for Students, Educators, and Parents
by Ian K. Macgillivray

Kicked Out
edited by Sassafras Lowrey and Jennifer Clare Burke

Out Law: What LGBT Youth Should Know about Their Legal Rights
by Lisa Keen

GLBTQ: The Survival Guide for Queer and Questioning Teens
by Kelly Huegel

Growing Up Gay in America: Informative and Practical Advice for Teen Guys
by Jason R. Rich

Questioning Their Sexuality and Growing Up Gay
by Jason R. Rich

Free Your Mind: The Book for Gay, Lesbian, and Bisexual Youth—and Their Allies
by Ellen Bass and Kate Kaufman

Come Out and Win: Organizing Yourself, Your Community, and Your World
by Sue Hyde

Coming Out, Coming In: Nurturing the Well-Being and Inclusion of Gay Youth in Mainstream Society
by Linda Goldman

Sex: A Book for Teens: An Uncensored Guide to Your Body, Sex, and Safety
by Nikol Hasler

Intersex (For Lack of a Better Word)
by Thea Hillman

Intersex
by Catherine Harper

HISTORICAL

Becoming Visible: A Reader in Gay and Lesbian History for High School and College Students
edited by Kevin Jennings

Completely Queer: The Gay and Lesbian Encyclopedia
by Steve Hogan

The Meaning of Matthew: My Son's Murder in Laramie, and a World Transformed
by Judy Shepard

Odd Girls and Twilight Lovers: A History of Lesbian Life in Twentieth-Century America
by Lillian Faderman

Stonewall
by Martin B. Duberman

Stonewall: The Riots That Sparked the Gay Revolution
by David Carter

Transgender Warriors: Making History, from Joan of Arc to Dennis Rodman
by Leslie Feinberg

Gay America: Struggle for Equality
by Linas Alsenas

FICTION AND ANTHOLOGIES

50 Ways of Saying Fabulous
by Graeme Aitken
Growing up on a remote farm in New Zealand can be really gay.

Awkward and Definition: The High School Comic Chronicles of Ariel Schrag
by Ariel Schrag
This is Schrag's graphic memoir of her freshman and sophomore years as a lesbian teen.

Baby Be-Bop
by Francesca Lia Block
This urban fairy-tale is about a 16-year-old gay boy in Los Angeles.

Boy Meets Boy
by David Levithan
Imagine gay teen love in a fantasy world where homophobia doesn't exist.

Calico
by Dorien Grey
Young cowboys discover romance in the mountains.

Drama Queers!
by Frank Anthony Polito
A high school senior in the 1980s has drama club adventures.

Deliver Us From Evie
by M. E. Kerr
Being queer in a rural town is not easy.

Empress of the World
by Sara Ryan
A story of lesbian love is set in a summer program for gifted teens.

The Full Spectrum: A New Generation of Writing About Gay, Lesbian, Bisexual, Transgender, Questioning, and Other Identities
edited by David Levithan and Billy Merrell
This anthology of poems, stories, and diary entries is by LGBT adults.

Geography Club
by Brent Hartinger
Contemporary teens navigate high school in this hilarious and hair-raising novel.

The House You Pass on the Way
by Jacqueline Woodson
Kathy's favorite lesbian teen book is about a 14-year-old girl growing up in a rural southern community.

Keeping You a Secret
by Julie Anne Peters
A transfer student attracts the attention of a high school senior when she attempts to start a queer support group.

Kissing Kate
by Lauren Myracle
What happens when best girlfriends kiss?

Maurice
by E. M. Forster
Marke's favorite novel is about young British university students discovering their gay desires.

The Necessary Hunger
by Nina Revoyr
When their parents fall in love, two star high school basketball players are thrown together.

Not the Only One: Lesbian and Gay Fiction for Teens
edited by Jane Summer
A fiction anthology

Parrotfish
by Ellen Wittlinger
A transgender teen struggles for acceptance.

Rainbow Boys
by Alex Sanchez
Three gay teens find friendship and more with each other.

Reflections of a Rock Lobster: A Story about Growing Up Gay
by Aaron Fricke
This memoir relates one of the first fights to bring a same-sex date to the prom.

Rubyfruit Jungle
by Rita Mae Brown
This is still one of the brashest, funniest coming of age novels ever published.

How I Paid for College: A Novel of Sex, Theft, Friendship & Musical Theater
By Marc Acito
Crime doesn't pay. Or does it?

COMICS

Pride High series
by Tommy Roddy
This is the story of a GSA at a high school for youth with super powers.

Tough Love: High School Confidential
by Abby Denson
Read about teen boys in love, Japanese manga style.

Index

About the Authors

Kathy Belge co-authored the book *Lipstick & Dipstick's Essential Guide to Lesbian Relationships* and writes on lesbian life for *Curve* magazine and About.com. She has worked extensively with queer youth and was the director of the Sexual Minority Youth Resource Center, Oregon's largest program for LGBT teens. Kathy lives in Portland, Oregon.

Marke Bieschke is the former health and dating editor of Gay.com and PlanetOut.com and a current Senior Editor at the *San Francisco Bay Guardian.* He has also spoken about gay issues on National Public Radio and CBS radio. Marke lives in San Francisco, California.

About the Artist

Christian Robinson loves to make things. Born and raised in Los Angeles, California, he received a BFA in character animation from the California Institute of the Arts and has interned with Pixar Animation Studios and the Sesame Street Workshop. He currently works as a freelance artist and lives in San Francisco, California.

About the Teen Advisors

The following teens served as advisors on *Queer*.

Sara Balabanlilar, 17, is a junior at Bellaire High School in Houston, Texas. She is the happy president of the GSA at her school and plans to spend her life reading philosophy books, drinking green tea, and being a LGBTQ activist.

Anna Livia Chen, 14, is a freshman at Mountain View High in California. She is the outreach coordinator at her current GSA and started her own GSA at her middle school in 8th grade. When she's not kayaking or playing guitar, Anna Livia devotes her time to activism and hopes to make the world a better place, one person at a time.

Danielle Dokes, 16, is a sophomore at El Cerrito High School in California. She is a part of the GSA at her school as well as the Rainbow Clique, a group for queer youth educators and activists. She has also been a public speaker for the nonprofit LGBT organization Ally Action. She plans to study sociology in college.

Danny Vanity, 18, is a junior at Skyline High School in Oakland, California. He is a proud member of the LGBTQ community. He is also a member of the Queer Youth Leadership Camp (QYLC), an organization started by UC Berkeley students, and his high school's GSA.

Alex Weick, 17, is a junior at Belmont High School in Belmont, Massachusetts. He runs the school's GSA as well as the Feminist Alliance and is a registered speaker for Greater Boston's chapter of Parents, Families, and Friends of Lesbians and Gays (PFLAG).

Kathy's Acknowledgments

Thanks to all of the LGBT youth I have worked with over the years who have inspired me, educated me, and pushed me into this life's work that I love.

Thanks to my niece Erika and to my sister Mary for their suggestions and insights; to my friends and family for their support and encouragement; and to Gina Daggett for reminding me that dreams can come true. I'd also like to especially thank my co-author Marke Bieschke; Deborah Brosseau, the amazing publicist who introduced me to Zest Books; my editor Karen Macklin; and everyone at Zest.

Marke's Acknowledgments

Thanks to my parents, family, and friends for always accepting and supporting me; my fiancé David for his advice and encouragement; the amazing queer teens who offered feedback and welcomed questions about their lives; my co-author Kathy Belge for a wonderful writing experience, and Karen Macklin and the folks at Zest for believing in the power of young people.